What Must I Do To be Saved, Lord?

THE GREAT QUESTION

Dr. Ohene Aku Kwapong

What Must I Do to be Saved, Lord?

THE GREAT QUESTION

All rights reserved. No part of this book may be reproduced in any form without written permission from Songhai Publishing, except in the case of brief quotations embodied in articles and reviews.

THE ANCIENT PROPHETS MANDATE SERIES

ISBN: 978-1-0878-7146-2

Copyright © 2021, 2025 inCHRIST - A PUBLICATION OF SONGHAI PUBLISHING

DEDICATION

To the memory of all the men and women, who have labored, with compassion and strength of heart to help many put into practice the simple wisdom of God and the words of Jesus, and to all those who desire love for God and faithfulness to his written word.

To the memory of my loving sister, Constance Offeibea Kwapong.

As Jesus was saying these things, a woman in the crowd called out, "Blessed is the mother who gave you birth and nursed you." He replied, "Blessed rather are those who hear the word of God and obey it."

Table of Contents

Why do I need to be saved? 3

    The Ox knows its master. 9
    A call to make ready a people prepared for the Lord. 13
    What does repentance mean? 17
    This is my son; with him, I am well pleased. 21

Where do we begin? 25

    A sound doctrine or false doctrine 29

An advice worth your soul 47

    Contextomy 48

Who is this Jesus? 57

    The Kingdom of God 72
    The Church 89
    His Final Instruction 104

What Peter & the Apostles taught 107

    Jesus' final instruction to the 11 apostles 123
    Conversions in the First Church 131

Paul and the troubled waters 155

    Paul's Conversion: Obedience, Not Abstraction 157

    PAUL'S moment of decision 166
    Paul and the Problem of Denominations 170

What must I do to be saved, Lord? 187

    The Kerygma of the Early Church 188
    God's Expectation 191
    The written word of God 193
    The First Decision point 211
    The Second Decision point 214
    The Third Decision point 216
    False Doctrines 218
    When all is said and done 245

Appendix 252

On the Physical Death of Jesus Christ 252

References 274

HE THAT HATH EAR

We, too, approach the gospel with preconceptions. Our cultural lenses, religious backgrounds, and personal desires all shape what we're ready to hear. But Jesus doesn't call us to passive agreement. He calls us to allegiance—to trust and obedience, the kind born not of religious habit but of a heart reshaped by grace and truth.

To this end, another parable speaks with particular force:

> "There was one man who had two sons. And he approached the first, and said, my son, go work today in my vineyard. But he answered and said, I will not do so: but after that, he repented and went. And he approached the second and said likewise. And he answered and said, I will go, my master, but he went not. Which of these two, did the father's will? They answered Him, The first. And Jesus said to them: Truly I tell you, that the transgressors and harlots go before you, into the Kingdom of Heaven." (Matthew 21:28–31)

This is a stunning moment. Jesus is not simply offering moral advice. He is announcing that the kingdom of God is arriving in and through him—and that those long thought excluded are rushing in ahead of the supposedly righteous. Why? Because they heard, repented, and followed.

It is not enough to say we believe. What matters is whether our lives reflect the truth we claim. In a world that too often equates faith with private spirituality or inherited religion, Jesus confronts us with a sharper demand: Will we recognize his authority—not as a human construct, but as the very voice of God, come at last to restore and renew?

This book, then, is not a mere theological treatise. It is an invitation—to rediscover the gospel of the kingdom as Jesus preached it, to allow our assumptions to be challenged, and to enter the life of obedience that flows from faith.

The apostle Paul, writing to his young protégé, put it plainly:

> *"Watch your life and doctrine closely. Persevere in them, because if you do, you will save both yourself and your hearers."* (1 Timothy 4:16)

So, take heart. Examine again the words of Jesus. Let them confront, comfort, and commission you. And above all, have the courage to obey.

In Christ's service,

Ohene Aku Kwapong

1

Why do I need to be saved?

WHAT MUST I DO TO BE SAVED?

Roughly five centuries before Jesus strode across the Galilean hills proclaiming that the kingdom of God was at hand, another great spiritual figure, Shakyamuni—known also as Gautama Siddhartha—voiced a longing that resonates deeply with the heart of the human story: *"At all times I think to myself: How can I cause living beings to gain entry into the unsurpassed way and quickly acquire the body of a Buddha?"* His was a cry born of compassion, of a desire to see humanity restored to its fullest potential.

And Siddhartha was not alone in this longing. Long before him, patriarchs like Abraham, and philosophers among the Greeks who came after, pondered the same questions: *What does it mean to live well? What is the purpose of our lives? How can we flourish as human beings?*

This quest is not foreign to Scripture. Indeed, the Bible tells a story of a God who creates humanity in his own image—not as mere cogs in a cosmic machine, but as wise stewards, image-bearers called to reflect God's character into the world and to reflect the praises of creation back to its Creator. But with that gift came freedom, and with freedom came the tragic possibility of rebellion. The result is not merely moral failure, but a distortion of our very vocation—leading to behaviors that deface God's world, fracture relationships, and tear at the fabric of creation itself.

The ancient Hebrew Scriptures, especially through the Mosaic Law, serve as both mirror and guide—revealing the consequences of humanity's choices while calling God's people to a different way, a holy way. And even deeper than Law lies the inner compass of conscience—God's gracious whisper in every human soul. Yet this too is often dulled, ignored, or bent to our own ends.

We are born, it seems, with the deep-seated assumption that we know what life is for, that we can find our own path. But life has a way of upending our certainties. As we grow, suffer, hope, and strive, the illusions fade, and the deeper questions rise again. Many begin a search—sometimes quietly, sometimes desperately—for meaning, for wholeness, for God.

The remarkable claim of the New Testament is this: that the God who had spoken in many ways—through prophets, through creation, through conscience and covenant—has now spoken decisively and definitively through his Son. In Jesus of Nazareth, we are not given merely a better teacher or a wiser path, but the living embodiment of Israel's God come in person. In him, we see (1) what it means to be truly human, and (2) what it takes to live in faithful relationship with our Creator.

Jesus doesn't offer a generic spirituality or a disembodied salvation. He brings to completion the story that began with Abraham, the vocation to bless the nations, to restore not only human hearts but the whole creation. For as the great religions have rightly sensed, humanity's relationship with the earth is not incidental—it is integral. When we live in line with our true calling, creation itself flourishes. When we rebel, it groans under the weight of our missteps.

Nowhere is God's heartbreak over this more vividly displayed than in the opening oracle of the prophet Isaiah. Speaking not only to ancient Israel but to the condition of all humanity, Isaiah records God's cry:

> *"Hear, O heavens! Listen, O earth! For the LORD has spoken:*
> *'I reared children and brought them up, but they have*

> *rebelled against me. The ox knows his master, the donkey his owner's manger, but Israel (mankind) does not know, my people do not understand.'*
>
> *Ah, sinful nation, a people loaded with guilt, a brood of evildoers, children given to corruption! They have forsaken the LORD; they have spurned the Holy One of Israel and turned their backs on him.*
>
> *Why should you be beaten anymore? Why do you persist in rebellion?*
>
> *Your whole head is injured, your whole heart afflicted. From the sole of your foot to the top of your head there is no soundness—only wounds and welts and open sores, not cleansed or bandaged or soothed with oil."*
>
> (Isaiah 1:2–6)

This is not merely condemnation—it is lament. It is the cry of a Father grieving the ruin of his children, the sorrow of a Creator watching his masterpiece unravel.

And yet, woven through the sorrow is hope. For in Jesus the Messiah, God has not abandoned the project. On the contrary, he has taken upon himself the wound, the rebellion, the sorrow—and through the cross and resurrection, inaugurated a new creation. The call now is not merely to feel remorse, but to return, to repent, and to walk in the newness of life made possible through him.

The question, then, is not whether humanity seeks meaning—but whether we will recognize the one who is the Way, the Truth, and the Life. The next two tables that follow capture the timeline of that search for meaning throughout the history of humankind.

WHAT MUST I DO TO BE SAVED?

Timeline of Religions and Search for Meaning

	POPULATION	INFLUENCERS	SHAMAISM	HINDUISM	JUDAISM	BUDDHISM	CONFUSCIUS	CHRISTIANITY	ISLAM
12,000		Shamanism / Animism							
3000 - 1000	14 million - 50 million	Lord Sri Krishna in 3112 BCE. Narmer (also known as Menes)							
600									
500		Confucious 551-479 BC							
450		Gautam Siddartha 480-400 BC							
400 - 300		Socrates 469-399 BC / Aristotle 384-322 BC					Confucianism, Taoism		
1	170 million	Jesus 2 BC - 33 CE							
50 - 100									
400		Dionysius Exiguus, Christian monk invents the AD/BC Calendar system							
500	190 million	Tientai, Chinese Budhist Teacher 538 - 596 CE	Shamanism	Hinduism	Judaism	Buddhism		Christianity	
1000 - 1200	254 million	Mohammed / Ali Ibn Abi Talib (Sufism)							
1300		Nichiren Daishonin the Buddha of True Causes, Latter Day of the Law and founder of Nichiren Buddhism is born, 1222							
1500	435 million								Islam
1600		English Separatist John Smyth, 1609 (Baptist)					Shintoism	Baptist	
1700		John Calvin, John Knox etc						Calvinism, Presbyteranism	
1800		• Joseph Smith (Mormonism) • William Miller, Joseph Bates (Seventh Day Adventist)						Mormonism, Seventh Day Adventist	Ahmadiyya Islam (Punjab, India)
1900		• Charles Parham, William Seymour (Pentecostalism) • Charles T Russel (Jehovah Witnesses)						Pentecostalism, Jehovah Witnesses	Bahá'Y Faith (Iran)
2000	6080 million	L. Ron Hubbard (Scientology)						Scientology	

WHAT MUST I DO TO BE SAVED?

History of the Search

BC / AD	INFLUENCERS	HOLY BOOKS	RELIGION
12,000	Shamaism / Animism	Oral Belief Systems	Shamaism / Animism
3000 - 1000	Lord Sri Krishna in 3112 BCE Narmer (also known as Menes)	The Pyramid Texts, are composed in Ancient Egypt 2494–2345 BCE Hindu Sacred Scripture Bhagavad Gita Upanishads & Veda	• Hindu Trinity • Hieroglyphic was one of the first complete scripts to be used in ancient Egypt. • Temple of Karnak built in 1900 BCE • Vedas Sacred Texts (Vedism) • Hebrew Bible (Tanakh) • Daoism (Chinese) - fate is controlled by deities and ancestor worship 1700 - 1100 BC
600		The Torah (also Oral Torah)	Torah - The Pentateuch (5 books of Moses created)
500	Confucious 551-479 BC	Oral Torah	Kong Fuzi (Confucius) was born, philosophy of respect and tradition - 551-479 BCE
450	Gautam Siddartha 480-400 BC	Tannak (Torah, Neviim, Ketuvim)	The Sutras and The Lotus Sutra Gautam Siddartha, the Buddha, founder of Buddhism dies, 480 BCE
400 - 300	Socrates 469-399 BC Aristotle 384-322 BC		Aristotle publishes the Organon, the universe has always existed
1 AD	Jesus 2 BC - 33 CE		Third Buddhist council, 250 BCE
50 - 100		Letters of Apostles, Gospels The New Testament written around 150 AD, and some scholars would date them all to no later than 70 AD or 80 AD.	Christian Council of Jerusalem is held, 50-60
400	Dionysius Exiguus, Christian monk invents the AD /BC Calendar system	Contantine commisions creation of 5 Bibles	• First Ecumenical Council, Council of Nicaea is convened to attain a consensus on doctrine, Nicene Creed, 325 • Second Ecumenical Council, the Council of Constantinople, reaffirms the Nicene Creed repudiating Arianism and Macedonianism. • Constantine legalizes Christianity, Constantine I proclaims religious freedom in Roman Empire in the Edict of Milan, 313 • St. Augustine of Hippo writes his confessions, 397-398
500	Tientai, Chinese Budhist Teacher 538 - 596 CE	Kojiki, Nohon Shoki	The Synod of Hippo, council of bishops of early Christianity listed and approved a biblical canon, 393
1000 - 1200	Mohammed Ali ibn Abi Talib (Sufism)	The Quran	• Quran was verbally revealed by God to Muhammad through the angel Gabriel • Mohammed performs the Hejira, his journey from Mecca to Medina, beginning of Muslim Era, 622 • Shia Muslims believe that just as a prophet is appointed by God alone, only God has the prerogative to appoint the successor to his prophet. They believe God chose Ali, Mohammed's first cousin. Sunnis think Abu Bakr his father in law is rightful successor
1300 - 1500	Nichiren Daishonin the Buddha of True Causes, Latter Day of the Law and founder of Nichiren Buddhism is born, 1222		• Henry VIII separates the English Church from Rome and takes the position of Supreme Head of the Church of England, 1534 • Luther nail his 95 Theses to the door of the Castle Church in Wittenberg, triggering the Reformation, 1517 CE • Edict of Nantes issued by Henri IV granting Protestants rights within Catholic France, 1593
1600 - 1700	English Separatist John Smyth, 1609 John Calvin, John Knox etc (Baptist)		• Rene Descartes writes his Meditations, 1641 • Galileo Galilei is excommunicated by the Church and imprisoned for life, for upholding that the Earth revolves around the Sun, 1633
1800	• Joseph Smith (Mormonism) • William Miller, Joseph Bates (Seventh Day Adventist)	The Book of Mormon	• Mirza Ghulam Ahmad founded Ahmadiya Islam in Punjab, India • 1870 1st Vatican Council • Joseph Smith (Mormonism) claims to have been given a book by angel Moroni 1805-1844 CE • William Miller started the Adventist movement. His followers became known as Millerites, 1830s
1900	• Charles Parham, William Seymour (Pentecostalism) • Charles T Russel (Jehovah Witnesses)	New World Bible (Jehovah Witness Translation)	• Jehovah Witnesses established, Charles Taze Russel, 1852 - 1916 CE • Pentecostalism established, Charles Parham, William Seymour, 1873 - 1929 CE • Siyyid 'Ali-Muhammad founded Baha'i Faith (1819-1850 CE)
2000	L. Ron Hubbard (Scientology)		Scientology established, L. Ron Hubbard, 1911-1986

The Ox knows its master.

One of the most striking observations about the created order is that everything—every creature, every living organism, every cosmic law—testifies silently yet powerfully to the One who made it. The stars do not need a sermon to shine forth the glory of God; the rivers do not hesitate in their course, nor the beasts forget their place in the order of creation. All creation, as Paul tells us in Romans 8, groans not in rebellion but in longing for the revealing of the sons and daughters of God.

And yet, the human story is painfully different. Of all the creatures in God's world, it is we who resist our vocation. Created in the very image of God, gifted with life, liberty, and love, we are also burdened with a freedom that can either glorify our Creator—or deny him altogether. And so often, we choose wrongly. We live in ways that fracture community, damage creation, and wound our very selves. In metaphor, as the prophets so often put it, our souls become riddled with sores, the kind that fester not only on the surface but deep in the interior spaces of our being. Life begins to rot from the inside out.

And yet, the tragedy is not just in the sin—it is in our failure to see it. We grow numb. Deception blinds us. We craft clever narratives to avoid facing the emptiness, the futility, the aching sorrow at the core of our existence. But God sees with unclouded vision. And what He sees, as recorded in the Scriptures, is far removed from what He intended. His heart breaks, not because He is vindictive, but because He is a Father whose children have run far from home.

The prophet Ezekiel gives voice to this divine grief through a parable—a raw, painful metaphor of two sisters, Oholah and Oholibah, representing Samaria and Jerusalem. Their story is one of tragic betrayal, idolatry, and the deep self-deception of spiritual infidelity:

> *"Son of man, there were two women, daughters of the same mother. They became prostitutes in Egypt... They were mine and gave birth to sons and daughters..."*

> *(Ezekiel 23:2-4)*

The narrative unfolds with graphic intensity. These women—once God's own—turn away in pursuit of foreign alliances, political idolatry, and cultural seduction. The lovers they chased, the gods they adopted, ultimately brought ruin, not renewal. The horror is not in the metaphor's vividness but in its truth. This is what covenant betrayal looks like. This is what happens when a people forget the God who called them, liberated them, and gave them a purpose.

> *"Because you have forgotten me and thrust me behind your back, you must bear the consequences of your lewdness and prostitution."*

> *(Ezekiel 23:35)*

God is not simply expressing moral outrage—He is exposing the broken relationship between Creator and creature. Israel, like humanity as a whole, had been planted like a choice vine, cultivated with care. But she became wild, twisted, corrupted. And the pain is mutual: creation groans, humanity suffers, and the heart of God mourns.

The prophetic witness is clear: outward appearances may deceive others, but the soul knows its own condition. Many may carry the illusion of success, strength, or spiritual confidence. But alone, in the stillness of the night, lying on the pillow of silence, the truth is often unbearable. Life without God becomes a burdensome fog—a mixture of sorrow, guilt, frustration, and alienation.

And yet—yet!—the message of Scripture is not ultimately one of condemnation but of invitation. For even amid judgment, God holds out the promise of restoration. Through the prophet Jeremiah, God issues a call not to punishment but to return:

> "Consider then and realize how evil and bitter it is for you when you forsake the LORD your God... Although you wash yourself with soda and use an abundance of soap, the stain of your guilt is still before me," declares the Sovereign LORD.

(Jeremiah 2:19, 2:22)

And then, a voice of mercy cuts through the sorrow:

> "Only acknowledge your guilt... 'Return, faithless people,' declares the LORD, 'for I am your husband. I will choose you... and bring you to Zion.'"

(Jeremiah 3:13–14)

Here is the gospel before the gospel. The cry of a wounded Creator becomes the call of a redeeming God. Like the father in Jesus' parable of the prodigal son, God runs toward the returning sinner with open arms. The question is not whether we are invited back—the question is whether we will respond.

This is where true salvation begins—not in ritual or appearance, but in the reorientation of the heart. A man or a woman becomes a true child of God not merely by identity, but by obedience. As the Scriptures make clear again and again, to belong to God is to trust Him, to walk in His ways, and to carry His image faithfully into the world.

That choice lies before each of us. Not in theory, but in practice. Not someday, but today.

A call to make ready a people prepared for the Lord.

The story of God's mission to restore creation is not a tale of distant power and detached divinity. It is, at its very core, a story of a God who longs to be with His people—a God whose providential desire is not simply to rule, but to relate. This yearning is voiced again and again in the Scriptures. And in the closing verses of the Old Testament, in the book of Malachi, a whisper of this divine initiative breaks through:

> "Behold, I will send you Elijah the prophet before the great and terrible day of the LORD comes."
>
> (Malachi 4:5)

This is no idle promise. It is the signal that the great divine drama is nearing its climax. For centuries, Israel had awaited the day when God would come in power, not just to judge, but to redeem; not only to expose sin, but to forgive it. That promise, spoken through Malachi, took on flesh in the wilderness through a strange and fiery figure named John.

John the Baptist didn't arise by accident. He was born into prophetic purpose, and his life was the hinge between the long hope of Israel and the dawning of the kingdom of God. The angel declared before his birth that he would go before the Lord "in the spirit and power of Elijah":

> *"To turn the hearts of the fathers to their children and the disobedient to the wisdom of the righteous—to make ready a people prepared for the Lord."*
>
> *(Luke 1:17)*

Indeed, John's appearance, clothed in camel's hair and leather (Mark 1:6), echoed the ancient prophet Elijah (2 Kings 1:8). But his mission was not merely to look like a prophet; it was to awaken the people of God. He was the advance guard of the coming King.

When John was born, his father Zechariah, filled with the Holy Spirit, prophesied the meaning of his son's life in words that have shaped the church's understanding of salvation ever since:

> *"You, my child, will be called a prophet of the Most High; for you will go on before the Lord to prepare the way for him, to give his people the knowledge of salvation through the forgiveness of their sins..."*
>
> *(Luke 1:76–77)*

This was something radically new. In Israel's long history, there had been temple sacrifices and covenant renewal, but here was a man proclaiming that the God of Israel was about to act in a fresh way—a decisive act of mercy, where forgiveness would no longer be confined to the rituals of the Temple but would be opened to all who repented and turned toward God's coming kingdom.

John's proclamation was simple yet revolutionary:

> "Repent, for the kingdom of God is near."

But we must not reduce that word "repent" to a mere moral scrubbing. In John's context—and indeed in Jesus' as well—repentance was about rethinking everything. It was about turning from false hopes and hollow loyalties, and orienting one's whole life toward God's coming reign. To "repent" meant to realign your story with God's story, to prepare not just the outer life, but the inner terrain of the heart for what God was about to do.

And when the people asked, "What should we do?"—John did not point them toward abstract religiosity. He gave earthy, ethical, kingdom-shaped answers:

> *"The man with two tunics should share with him who has none."*
>
> *"Don't collect any more than you are required to."*
>
> *"Don't extort money or accuse falsely; be content with your pay."*
>
> (Luke 3:10–14)

In other words, John was preparing a people whose hearts and hands were ready to receive Jesus. He wasn't simply baptizing for the sake of ritual purity—he was forging a community marked by justice, generosity, honesty, and mercy. This was the kind of soil into which the seed of the gospel could be planted. These were the hearts being readied for the Messiah.

We must not miss the shape of this message for our own time. God is still preparing people. And the call remains the same: repent—not out of fear, but out of hope. Not merely to avoid judgment, but to participate in the restoration that Jesus brings. The God who acted through John and fulfilled His promise in Jesus is still acting, still calling, still inviting.

The question remains: when the kingdom draws near, will we recognize it? Will we repent—not only in word, but in deed—and walk in the mercy and light of the coming King?

What does repentance mean?

At the heart of John the Baptist's message was not mere moral improvement nor abstract spirituality—it was the call to turn around, to reorient one's life entirely, to prepare for what God was about to do. The word we translate as repentance has been tragically flattened in modern usage. But in the world of Second Temple Judaism—and indeed, in the kingdom-message that Jesus and John both proclaimed—repentance meant nothing less than a radical reordering of life: a turning away from self-rule, and a turning toward the sovereignty, the kingship, the kingdom of God.

To repent, then, was to begin living as though God were truly in charge—to reconfigure one's behaviors, values, character, and community practices in line with God's justice and mercy. It meant acknowledging that God is not a distant deity, but the one who sends rain on the just and the unjust, who upholds the poor, who calls his people to imitate his generosity.

John's call to repentance carried practical implications. When the crowds asked, "What shall we do?"—they weren't handed a list of religious rituals. They were told, instead:

> *"If you have two tunics, give one to the person who has none."*
>
> *"If you have food, share it."*
>
> *"If you're a tax collector, don't exploit the system."*
>
> *"If you're a soldier, do no violence unjustly, and be content."*
>
> (Luke 3:10–14)

This is not peripheral. It is central. Repentance, for John, was not simply sorrow over sin—it was covenantal faithfulness, expressed in generosity, justice, and godliness. It was, as Paul would later say, the life of contentment and godliness, which has great gain (1 Timothy 6:6–7).

When John said, "Repent, for the kingdom of God is at hand," he was announcing that God's reign—His rule, His will being done on earth as in heaven—was on the brink of breaking in. Those who wished to participate in this new reality, this new exodus, had to undergo not only moral reform but relational realignment. They were to confess their sins and be baptized—not as a mere symbol, but as an embodied declaration that they were stepping into God's purposes.

But it is vital to understand what John's baptism was and what it was not. His immersion in the Jordan did not cause the forgiveness of sins. Rather, it marked the person as one who recognized their need for God's mercy and who acknowledged God's purpose for their life. As Luke's gospel clarifies:

> "All the people, even the tax collectors, when they heard Jesus' words, acknowledged that God's way was right, because they had been baptized by John. But the Pharisees and experts in the law rejected God's purpose for themselves, because they had not been baptized by John."
>
> (Luke 7:29–30)

Here we find a stark line: to accept John's baptism was to accept God's purpose. To reject it—even on the grounds of religious authority—was to resist the very movement of heaven.

John knew that his baptism was incomplete. He baptized with water, but he testified of one who would come after him, "mightier than I," who would baptize "with the Holy Spirit and with fire." In the symbolic world of first-century Judaism, water represented cleansing and preparation. Fire represented finality—judgment, yes, but also purification. And the Holy Spirit, long promised through the prophets, would come as the very breath of new creation, the empowering presence of God dwelling in His people.

John's baptism, then, was preparatory. It was a signpost. It readied the people not just for forgiveness, but for transformation. For while the Scriptures are clear that "without the shedding of blood there is no forgiveness of sins" (Hebrews 9:22; Leviticus 17:11), Jesus—before the cross—demonstrated his divine authority to forgive sins (Luke 7:48). And after his death and resurrection, he would pour out the Spirit to accomplish what John could only begin: not just washing in water, but indwelling by God's own presence.

The tragedy, as always, was that those most outwardly religious often missed the moment. The Pharisees and teachers of the law, proud of their status and learning, could not accept the disruptive nature of John's call. They believed repentance could remain private. But John—and Jesus after him—insisted that true repentance must be embodied, must be visible, must result in a changed life and a new allegiance.

Rejecting John's baptism wasn't simply a ritual omission. It was, according to Luke, a rejection of God's very purpose for their lives.

This is the great reversal at the heart of the gospel: the kingdom does not come through power, pride, or piety, but through humility, confession, and the readiness to step into the waters of change. The call of heaven demands a response—and that response is obedience.

To ignore it is not simply to walk a different religious path—it is to reject the invitation of the God who longs to rescue, restore, and renew.

This is my son; with him, I am well pleased.

As John stood in the Jordan, waist-deep in the waters of repentance, he had no idea that the Messiah he had been sent to reveal was already in his midst. He knew Jesus, yes—as a relative perhaps, a quiet and righteous man—but he did not yet know who Jesus truly was. That revelation would come not through whispered intuition or theological speculation, but through a moment of divine unveiling.

When Jesus came to be baptized, John resisted. "I need to be baptized by you—and do you come to me?" (Matthew 3:14). This was no mere expression of humility. John knew enough of God's holiness to sense that Jesus, unlike the rest, had no sin to confess. And yet, Jesus insisted. "Let it be so now; it is proper for us to do this to fulfill all righteousness."

In that moment, Jesus aligned himself with the obedient people of God—not standing apart from them, but plunging into their story, their baptism, their calling. And as he rose from the water, heaven tore open. The Spirit descended like a dove. A voice declared:

> *"This is my Son, whom I love; with him I am well pleased."*
>
> (Matthew 3:16–17)

Here, at last, was the long-awaited anointed one, and John knew it. As he later testified:

> *"I myself did not know him, but the one who sent me to baptize with water told me, 'The man on whom you see the*

> Spirit come down and remain is the one who will baptize with the Holy Spirit.' I have seen and I testify that this is the Son of God."
>
> (John 1:33–34)

If Jesus had not stepped into those waters, John would not have seen the sign. The crowds would have missed the moment. The kingdom would have remained veiled a little longer. But Jesus, in obedience to the call of righteousness, entered the waters of repentance—not because he needed to repent, but because this was what it meant to be the obedient Son. Just as he would later humble himself to the point of death—death on a cross—so now, he humbles himself beneath John's hand, submitting to the prophetic call of heaven (Philippians 2:5–8).

Why did he do it? The answer lies in Jesus' own words later on, when he asked his critics:

> "Was John's baptism from heaven, or from men?"
>
> (Luke 20:4)

Jesus saw John's baptism as heaven's initiative—part of the unfolding plan of God's rescue operation for the world. He obeyed not because he had to, but because he chose to, in order to fulfill what covenant faithfulness required.

And no sooner had he been baptized than the Spirit drove him into the wilderness. There, for forty days, Jesus confronted the dark spiritual forces that had corrupted Israel's story and distorted humanity's vocation. The devil did not simply tempt Jesus to break commandments—he attempted to call into question Jesus' identity: "If you are the Son of God..."

But Jesus would not bend. In his responses, he reveals three enduring truths for all who would follow him:

- Life is sustained not only by food, but by every word that proceeds from the mouth of God.
- Only God is to be worshipped, for He alone gives life and purpose.
- Faithfulness to God must never be confused with testing God's patience or power.

In the desert, the Son stood where Adam had fallen, where Israel had wandered, and where we so often stumble—and he stood firm. If he had failed there, the entire salvation project would have come undone. But he did not. He emerged as the faithful Israelite, the new Adam, the obedient Son.

Everything turns on this: Jesus is the Son of God. Not by human origin—not born of man's will—but conceived by the power of God. And yet, this foundational truth was lost on many of the religious leaders of the day. Why? Because, as Jesus said, they neither knew the Scriptures nor the power of God (Matthew 22:29). They were bound not by obedience, but by presumption—failing to recognize that the kingdom of heaven does not come to those who believe themselves already righteous, but to those who humble themselves in faith and obedience.

Even now, this remains the dividing line. Some recognize Jesus as the Son of God through long study, deep reflection, and surrender. Others are struck by the witness of Scripture or the sheer weight of

God's presence in their lives. And many, tragically, turn away—not because the evidence is lacking, but because their hearts are not open to the power of God nor formed by the narrative of His Word.

But the Scriptures are clear: the road to salvation begins with the acknowledgment that Jesus is the Son of God. It begins with the question: Do I believe this—and if I do, does my life reflect it? Our deepest beliefs are not what we write on paper but what we live and speak with conviction. If you speak freely about your favorite team, your music, your politics—do you speak, with equal clarity and joy, about the One you claim is Lord?

Jesus being the Son of God is not a theological abstraction. It is the heartbeat of the gospel, the hinge of history, and the beginning of new life. And with that truth comes the call—not merely to believe, but to repent, to realign, to follow. If Jesus is the Son of God, then his way must become your way, and his words must shape your life.

2

Where do we begin?

Suppose, for a moment, someone were to approach you, as they did Jesus or the apostles, and ask: "What must I do to be saved?" How would you respond? Would your answer resonate with the voice of Scripture—or would it reflect a version of the gospel more shaped by the echo chambers of denominational tradition, or the theological shorthand picked up in passing from church life? Would your answer bear the hallmark of the early Christian proclamation, the apostolic witness to the risen Lord? Or might it be, unintentionally perhaps, a gospel of your own invention?

We must be honest: if our answers to this foundational question are not grounded in the coherent witness of the New Testament, then either we have not fully understood the question—or worse, we risk having misunderstood the gospel itself.

This question—"What must I do to be saved?"—has echoed through the centuries, from the lips of the Philippian jailer (Acts 16:30) to countless men and women today who sense, however dimly, that the world is broken, and they are too, and that somehow God's rescue is both needed and near. Tragically, those who turn to the church for an answer often find a cacophony of conflicting voices. The result? A spiritual restlessness, a wandering from community to community in search of the clarity that eludes them, or a quiet disillusionment that eventually leads them away from the very hope they sought.

And yet the apostle Paul, writing to the church in Ephesus, leaves no room for confusion:

> *"There is one body and one Spirit, just as you were called to one hope when you were called; one Lord, one faith, one*

> *baptism; one God and Father of all, who is over all and through all and in all."*
>
> — *Ephesians 4:4–6*

In other words, if the church is the people of the one God, called in the name of the one Lord Jesus, animated by the one Spirit, then there must also be one faith—one gospel of salvation. Not many. Not a variety. Not a marketplace of spiritual remedies.

The multiplicity of answers offered today is not a sign of healthy diversity, but of tragic distortion. The gospel has too often been treated not as the royal announcement of the crucified and risen Messiah but as a set of personalized prescriptions—each tailored to the needs, fears, or preferences of the age. Churches, like misguided pharmacists, sometimes take the physician's prescription and alter it to suit their own assumptions. But when we tinker with the prescription, the patient does not heal. And in our age, the sickness of the world is painfully evident.

This, of course, is not a modern problem. Paul dealt with precisely this in his letter to the Galatians—a letter filled with pastoral anguish and apostolic urgency:

> *"Evidently some people are throwing you into confusion and are trying to pervert the gospel of Christ. But even if we or an angel from heaven should preach a gospel other than the one we preached to you, let them be under God's curse!"*
>
> — *Galatians 1:7–9*

Strong words, yes. But necessary. For Paul knew that to preach a different gospel was not simply a theological error—it was a betrayal of the Messiah himself. The gospel is not a message we are free to adjust. It is news we are summoned to announce: that Jesus, Israel's Messiah and the world's true Lord, has died for our sins, been raised from the dead, and now invites all people into a new life in him.

Hebrews, too, underscores the weight of this announcement:

> "How shall we escape if we ignore so great a salvation? This salvation, which was first announced by the Lord, was confirmed to us by those who heard him. God also testified to it by signs, wonders and various miracles, and gifts of the Holy Spirit distributed according to his will."
>
> — Hebrews 2:3-4

In other words, the message of salvation was not invented by the apostles; it was inaugurated by Jesus himself, confirmed by those who walked with him, and sealed by the living presence of the Spirit in the life of the early church.

And so, in what follows, we must do precisely what the New Testament itself teaches us to do: begin with Jesus—what he said, what he taught, what he embodied. Then we look to his apostles, who were commissioned not to innovate but to proclaim. And finally, we turn to Paul, that tireless herald of the gospel among the Gentiles, who was not teaching a new message but bearing the same truth into new territory.

The question is not simply: "What must I do to be saved?" but rather, "What is the salvation God has accomplished in Jesus—and how do I live in light of it?" When we recover that fuller, deeper vision, the gospel is no longer a formula for afterlife assurance, but the transforming news that God's kingdom has broken in through Jesus Christ—and that we are invited, by grace, into its new reality.

A sound doctrine or false doctrine

One of the most sobering moments in the entire teaching of Jesus comes at the close of the Sermon on the Mount, when he declares with unsettling clarity that not everyone who cries out "Lord, Lord" will enter the kingdom of heaven. It is not the verbal confession, however fervent, that assures one's standing in God's new world. Rather, it is the life shaped by obedience to the will of the Father—the life that embodies the teaching, the life that builds its foundation on rock.

> *"Not everyone who says to me, 'Lord, Lord,' will enter the kingdom of heaven, but only the one who does the will of my Father who is in heaven."*
>
> *— Matthew 7:21 (NIV)*

These words strike at the heart of a widespread misconception: that external displays of religious power or success—prophecy, exorcism, miraculous signs—can serve as sufficient evidence of genuine discipleship. Jesus anticipates the tragic surprise of many who, on the day of reckoning, will discover that their works, however dramatic, were not rooted in faithful obedience. They mistook the appearance of spirituality for the substance of the kingdom.

This is not to deny that Jesus' ministry was indeed accompanied by signs and wonders—far from it. But the heart of his teaching, the agenda he sets forth in the Sermon on the Mount and throughout the Gospels, is about becoming the kind of person through whom the reign of God quietly but powerfully comes to birth. Those who put Jesus' words into practice are not merely admiring a great teacher—they are stepping into the life of the new creation.

> *"Everyone who hears these words of mine and puts them into practice is like a wise man who built his house on the rock."*
>
> — *Matthew 7:24 (NIV)*

The contrast could not be more vivid. The wise build on the solid foundation of Jesus' teaching, shaped by his vision of God's kingdom. The foolish, however, build on sand—on shifting opinions, on half-truths dressed up as doctrine, or on the assumption that sincerity is a substitute for obedience. When the storm comes—and it always does—it is the house built on the words of Jesus, rightly heard and faithfully lived, that stands firm.

In our modern context, we must resist the temptation to reduce the Bible to a collection of subjective interpretations. The popular refrain—"Well, that's just your interpretation"—has become a way of sidestepping the hard edges of Jesus' teaching. But this is precisely the kind of self-deception that Jesus warns about. When the foundation is not his words but our assumptions about them, we are already building on sand.

Jesus' words are not given as helpful advice or abstract ideals; they are the blueprint for life in God's new world. His instruction is not merely "religious content" to be filed alongside other philosophies—it is the very will of God made flesh, a call to embody in our lives the very kingdom he announced.

And so, we must ask: are we building on the rock? Are we truly putting Jesus' teaching into practice, or are we content with religious activity that only bears a passing resemblance to the obedience he calls for? To live out Jesus' teaching is not a matter of checking boxes, nor is it a private spirituality detached from communal and ethical life. It is about aligning one's whole being with the kingdom way of being human that Jesus inaugurates.

The apostle Paul, with his deep pastoral concern, foresaw the danger of distortion even among those within the community of faith. In his farewell to the elders in Ephesus, he warned of the coming of those who would twist the message—not for the glory of God, but to gather followers for themselves:

> *"I know that after I leave, savage wolves will come in among you and will not spare the flock. Even from your own number men will arise and distort the truth in order to draw away disciples after them."*
>
> —Acts 20:29–30 (NIV)

This warning echoes with urgency today. In a culture where moral and doctrinal clarity is often blurred, and where charismatic personalities can sometimes overshadow the message of Jesus himself, the call to vigilance is more necessary than ever. Paul's own ministry was marked by tears—anguish over the prospect of God's people being led astray not by outright denial of Christ, but by subtle deviations from the truth he revealed.

At the heart of it all is this: Jesus has told us what it means to live in his kingdom. He has not left us in the dark. The only sure foundation—the only assurance we have of standing firm when the storm comes—is to build our lives on what he has actually said and done. Not on what merely sounds Christian, not on what is popular or palatable, but on the words of the one who loved us and gave himself for us, and now reigns as Lord over all.

Take one look at the contemporary Christian landscape and the fragmentation is unmistakable. Denominations abound. Doctrines diverge. Leaders with vast followings often teach conflicting messages. And yet—this cannot be what Jesus intended. The one who prayed that his followers would be one, as he and the Father are one (John 17:21), surely did not envisage the present confusion. Jesus proclaimed a single gospel, the arrival of God's kingdom through his life, death, and resurrection. So how have we arrived at such a multiplicity of doctrines, many of which contradict one another?

My friend, we must not be naïve. There is such a thing as truth, and there is such a thing as falsehood. And in the realm of what we call "Christendom," the distinction still matters. From the very beginning of the Christian movement, the apostles recognized the danger of distortion. Paul's letters to Timothy are a poignant reminder that this threat was not just theoretical—it was real, and it was present even in the earliest churches.

> *"Paul, an apostle of Christ Jesus by the command of God our Savior and of Christ Jesus our hope, to Timothy my true son in the faith... Stay there in Ephesus so that you may command certain men not*

to teach false doctrines any longer... These promote controversies rather than God's work—which is by faith."

—*1 Timothy 1:1–4 (NIV)*

Paul's concern was pastoral as well as theological. Myths, genealogies, and speculative teachings might fascinate the mind, but they do not shape hearts toward God's purposes. They lead to empty debates rather than faithful obedience. These false teachers, confident in their assertions, had wandered from the heart of the gospel—a gospel grounded in love, purity of heart, and sincere faith.

"They want to be teachers of the law, but they do not know what they are talking about... the law is good if one uses it properly... for whatever else is contrary to the sound doctrine that conforms to the glorious gospel of the blessed God, which he entrusted to me."

—*1 Timothy 1:7–11 (NIV)*

Paul's phrase "sound doctrine" is not a technicality—it's shorthand for the healthy, life-giving teaching that grows from the soil of the gospel Jesus himself sowed. And Paul is emphatic: any teaching that deviates from the glorious gospel—the good news that God's kingdom has come through Israel's Messiah—is not only false; it is dangerous.

In fact, Paul doesn't hesitate to say that this pattern of deviation, distortion, and deception will continue. He speaks prophetically about a time—indeed, a time that seems all too familiar to us now—when some will turn from the truth entirely:

> *"The Spirit clearly says that in later times some will abandon the faith and follow deceiving spirits and things taught by demons."*
>
> —1 Timothy 4:1 (NIV)

This is not melodrama. It is a sober diagnosis of the spiritual condition of a church susceptible to falsehood because it has drifted from its foundation. These teachings may carry a veneer of piety—prohibitions on marriage, dietary restrictions, ascetic rules—but they are rooted not in the freedom of the gospel but in a distortion of it.

And so, in this work, we must take Paul's pastoral warning with the utmost seriousness. We will examine, not simply what has been taught, but what has been assumed in Christian circles—myths and half-truths that have quietly supplanted the teaching of Jesus and the apostolic witness. The goal is not mere polemic, but recovery—a rediscovery of the one true message entrusted to the Church: that Jesus, the crucified and risen Lord, is the world's rightful King, and that following him means not only calling him "Lord," but living as if he truly is.

As Paul told Timothy, the gospel he received was not his to adjust—it was something entrusted to him. We are stewards, not inventors, of the message. The challenge before us is to recognize the difference between doctrines that merely sound Christian, and those that actually align with the voice of the Messiah. Because the line between the two is not just a theological curiosity—it is the line between obedience and rebellion, between truth and deception, between life on the rock and a house built on sand.

In his final recorded words to Timothy—his beloved co-worker in the gospel—Paul stands at the brink of his own martyrdom and speaks with unmistakable urgency. He speaks not merely as an aging apostle, but as one who knows, with clarity born of suffering and faith, that the future of the church depends on her faithfulness to the truth.

> *"In the presence of God and of Christ Jesus, who will judge the living and the dead, and in view of his appearing and his kingdom, I give you this charge: Preach the Word... For the time will come when people will not put up with sound doctrine... they will gather around them a great number of teachers to say what their itching ears want to hear."*
>
> — *2 Timothy 4:1–3 (NIV)*

This warning strikes at the heart of a very modern predicament. We live in a time, as Paul foresaw, when many prefer palatable opinions over challenging truth. What matters to many today is not whether something is true, but whether it sounds good—whether it confirms what we already want to believe. That, Paul insists, is a sign not of mature faith, but of spiritual drift. And it is nothing new.

The problem is not merely doctrinal disagreement—it is disobedience masquerading as discernment. It is a refusal to submit to the sound instruction that conforms to the teaching of Jesus himself. Even when the truth is presented clearly from Scripture, it is often dismissed by those who have already set their hearts on more comfortable myths.

But Paul will not have it. He reminds Timothy that his role is not to entertain the crowds or affirm their preferences, but to preach the

Word—in season and out, when it's convenient and when it's not. He is to correct, to rebuke, and to encourage with patience and careful teaching. In other words, Timothy must hold the line—not to protect an institution, but to guard the gospel itself.

Paul had seen firsthand how easily things could unravel. He names individuals—Hymenaeus, Alexander, Philetus—not to shame them for personal failures, but to warn others of the consequences of turning from the truth. These were not outsiders. These were once fellow believers who, by abandoning the truth of the resurrection or indulging in speculative teachings, ended up shipwrecking their faith—and that of others.

> *"Their teaching will spread like gangrene... They say that the resurrection has already taken place, and they destroy the faith of some."*
>
> — *2 Timothy 2:17–18 (NIV)*

The church, Paul insists, must be vigilant. This vigilance is not legalism—it is covenantal faithfulness. The gospel is not a vague spiritual vibe; it is a specific announcement about Jesus as Israel's Messiah and the world's true Lord. To deviate from that is not a small matter. It is to risk obscuring the very means by which God rescues and restores his people.

Peter, too, issues a sobering echo of Paul's concern:

> *"But there were also false prophets among the people, just as there will be false teachers among you... Many will follow their shameful ways and will bring the way of truth into disrepute."*
>
> — *2 Peter 2:1–2 (NIV)*

These warnings are not meant to foster paranoia but discernment. They compel us to ask: How do we recognize false teaching? And more importantly: How do we remain faithful to what Jesus actually taught?

Paul gives Timothy a simple but profoundly important metric:

> *"If anyone teaches false doctrines and does not agree to the sound instruction of our Lord Jesus Christ... he is conceited and understands nothing."*
>
> —*1 Timothy 6:3-4 (NIV)*

This is the crux of the matter. Every doctrine—no matter how theological it sounds—must be measured against the clear teaching of Jesus himself. The standard for truth is not popular consensus, nor even theological tradition, but the living Word as revealed in Christ and faithfully passed on by his apostles.

False teachings often sound spiritual. They may even quote Scripture. But the question we must always ask is: Is this what Jesus actually taught? And if not, however appealing or widespread it may be, we must have the courage to turn away from it. We must, as Paul says, "guard what has been entrusted" to us—refusing to be drawn in by "what is falsely called knowledge" (1 Timothy 6:20).

This book, then, is not written to inflame controversy but to bring clarity. Together we will examine several of the myths that have misled many within the church—ideas that sound Christian but deviate from the heart of the gospel. Our aim is not merely to reject error, but to recover the truth that sets people free: the truth Jesus taught, the truth the apostles obeyed, the truth the early church proclaimed in the face of opposition.

And when it comes to the great question—What must I do to be saved?—we must return not to religious slogans, nor to inherited assumptions, but to the teaching of Jesus himself and to the apostolic witness that flowed directly from his commission.

The real question is not, "What do people say today?" but rather, "What did Jesus command?" What did the apostles teach? And, Is what I believe and practice actually aligned with that same truth?

Only then can we be sure we are not among those who have "turned aside to myths," but among those who have built their lives on the rock of Christ's unchanging Word.

One of the great challenges facing the church in every generation is the question of discernment—not merely recognizing what sounds Christian, but truly grasping what is of Christ. In our world today, where a thousand voices speak in the name of Jesus, we must return, again and again, to the words and ways of Jesus himself. For if we lose sight of his voice, all that remains are echoes of opinion.

Let me offer a simple but profound analogy—one that, like many of Jesus' parables, draws from the world of ordinary life. Imagine a patient who has gone to the doctor and been given a handwritten prescription. That prescription is not meant to be a suggestion; it is a precise instruction from one who knows what will bring healing. The patient takes it to the pharmacist, trusting the remedy will be filled exactly as written. But what if the pharmacist—through carelessness, poor training, or overconfidence—alters the prescription? Perhaps he changes the dosage, substitutes the medicine, or decides on his own how often it should be taken. The result? The patient remains ill—or worse, is poisoned by what was intended to heal.

This, sadly, is the state of much of the Christian world today. Many teachers and preachers, like careless pharmacists, have misread or altered the prescription. Often this is not done with malice, but with mistaken confidence in teachings inherited uncritically. The gospel Jesus preached becomes diluted or distorted, not always through denial, but through neglect, through failure to return to the source—to the very words and life of Jesus himself.

False doctrine often comes about not because of deliberate rebellion, but because over time the original message is blurred. A story from World War I serves well here. A captain, needing reinforcements, sent word down a line of trenches: "Send reinforcements, we are going to advance." But as the message passed from soldier to soldier, it morphed. By the time it reached headquarters, it was nonsensical: "Send fourpence, we're going to a dance." The problem was not just noise—it was the failure to verify the message. Each assumed what they heard was correct. This is how, generation by generation, doctrinal truths can drift so far from Jesus' original voice that the result is barely recognizable as gospel.

The Apostle Paul understood this danger. In his letters to Timothy, he warned repeatedly of those who had "shipwrecked their faith" by deviating from the truth (1 Timothy 1:18–20). He names names—not to shame, but to make the point plain: this is not theoretical. It is happening in the church. Some of these individuals were not outsiders but former co-laborers who had embraced distortions, perhaps sincerely, but with devastating results.

> *"Their teaching will spread like gangrene... they say that the resurrection has already taken place, and they destroy the faith of some."*
>
> —2 Timothy 2:17–18

And so, what do we do? We test the spirits. As the Apostle John writes:

> *"Dear friends, do not believe every spirit, but test the spirits to see whether they are from God."*
>
> —1 John 4:1 (NIV)

But how do we test? John gives us the criteria: the true spirit is the one that acknowledges Jesus Christ has come in the flesh—not merely that he existed, but that he came from God, and that his words carry divine authority.

Jesus himself was unambiguous about what this means. To acknowledge him is to obey him. To accept his message is to submit to his teaching. He says:

> *"There is a judge for the one who rejects me and does not accept my words; that very word which I spoke will condemn him at the last day."*
>
> —John 12:48 (NIV)

In other words, we cannot say we accept Jesus and then ignore what he said. To disregard his teachings is to reject the one who sent him—the living God. Luke captures it plainly in Jesus' words:

> *"Whoever listens to you listens to me; whoever rejects you rejects me; but whoever rejects me rejects him who sent me."*
>
> — *Luke 10:16 (NIV)*

This is the line in the sand: Any doctrine—however well-intentioned, however popular—that does not align with Jesus' own words is a false doctrine. And those who persist in rejecting his teachings, even while claiming his name, are aligning themselves with the spirit of the antichrist—not a sensational villain, but a real spiritual posture of opposition to Jesus' kingship.

As John writes:

> *"Who is the liar? It is whoever denies that Jesus is the Christ. Such a person is the antichrist—denying the Father and the Son."*
>
> — *1 John 2:22-23 (NIV)*

But perhaps the most subtle—and dangerous—form of false teaching today is what we might call "the Error of the Pharisee." These are teachings that appear Christian. They use familiar words. They are embedded in tradition. But they quietly replace the difficult, demanding commands of Jesus with more palatable ideas—doctrines that cost less, ask less, and appeal more. As Jesus warned the Pharisees:

> *"You have a fine way of setting aside the commands of God in order to observe your own traditions!"*
>
> — *Mark 7:9 (NIV)*

Let us take a familiar phrase: "You shall know the truth, and the truth shall set you free." How many times have we heard this? It is biblical. It sounds right. But in most churches, it has been lifted out of its context—and in doing so, it has been stripped of its power.

What Jesus actually said is found in John 8:31-32:

> *"To the Jews who had believed him, Jesus said, 'If you hold to my teaching, you are really my disciples. Then you will know the truth, and the truth will set you free.'"*
>
> —*John 8:31-32 (NIV)*

Freedom does not come from simply knowing truth, but from living in obedience to Jesus' words. Truth is not abstract—it is embodied in Jesus' life and teaching. And freedom comes not through passive belief, but through active discipleship.

Would you like me to continue this section into an exploration of the "Error of the Pharisee" as a chapter heading, or expand it into a study format for teaching or small group discussion?

To those who had already begun to believe in him, Jesus gave this clear, powerful condition:

> *"If you hold to my teaching, you are really my disciples. Then you will know the truth, and the truth will set you free."*
>
> —*John 8:31-32 (NIV)*

Not just knowing the truth, but holding to it—abiding in it, living in it, practicing it. That's what makes one a true disciple. And it is only from within that life of faithful obedience that truth can work its liberating power. The difference between this and the more commonly quoted version—"You will know the truth, and the truth will set you free"—is subtle, but it is no less than the difference between being healed and remaining sick, between walking in the light and stumbling in darkness, between the kingdom of God and the kingdom of self.

For too long, in too many places, the message of Jesus has been subtly reshaped into a religion of intellectual agreement or cultural inheritance. But Jesus didn't say, "If you intellectually agree with me, then you're my disciple." He said, "If you obey my teachings." As John later writes:

> "The man who says, 'I know him,' but does not do what he commands is a liar... Whoever claims to live in him must walk as Jesus did."
>
> —1 John 2:3–6 (NIV)

Let us be clear: freedom—the kind that Jesus offers—is not found in mere theological knowledge, or even in correct belief alone. It comes from practicing what Jesus taught. It's like being trapped in the weight of spiritual bondage or addiction: knowing the steps to recovery doesn't set you free; actually taking the steps does.

Salvation, then, is not simply about agreeing that Jesus exists or that the Bible is true. It is about surrendering our ways to his, reshaping our whole lives around the rhythm and reality of the kingdom he proclaimed.

This is why Jesus was so clear—and so direct—about the stakes:

> "Not everyone who says to me, 'Lord, Lord,' will enter the kingdom of heaven, but only the one who does the will of my Father who is in heaven."
>
> —Matthew 7:21 (NIV)

So, we must pay careful attention—not to what seems Christian, or what sounds religious, or even what many others believe—but to what Jesus actually said and did. As Proverbs wisely reminds us:

> *"There is a way that seems right to a man, but in the end it leads to death."*
>
> — *Proverbs 14:12 (NIV)*

Truth, as Jesus taught it, must not be measured by how agreeable it sounds, but by whether it leads to faithful obedience to God. The kingdom of God is not a matter of opinion, tradition, or inherited ritual—it is a matter of truth breaking in through Jesus, and of our response to that truth.

The apostles, for their part, took this seriously. Both Peter and Paul consistently emphasized that the final authority in all things is not ecclesiastical tradition or inherited doctrine, but Jesus' own words. Paul reminds Timothy:

> *"If anyone teaches false doctrines and does not agree to the sound instruction of our Lord Jesus Christ... he is conceited and understands nothing."*
>
> — *1 Timothy 6:3-4 (NIV)*

So, when we ask the question, What must I do to be saved?, it matters deeply whose answer we accept. It is not enough to quote a preacher, a denomination, or even a family tradition. We must ask: What did Jesus say? What did the apostles, who heard him firsthand, teach and practice?

You might think this should be simple—just read Jesus' words and do what he said. But as Scripture reveals, many will refuse to understand—not because the message is unclear, but because their hearts are hard. As Isaiah prophesied, and Jesus repeated:

> *"You will be ever hearing but never understanding... For this people's heart has become calloused."*
>
> *— Matthew 13:14-15 (NIV)*

The truth is, understanding the words of Jesus isn't just a matter of intellect. It is a matter of the heart—of humility, honesty, and a desire to please God rather than men. If our motives are pure, our ears will be open; but if we are seeking what sounds good or socially acceptable, we will miss the truth, even when it is right in front of us.

In the end, there are only two roads: the road of truth that leads to life, and the road of falsehood that leads to ruin. As Paul exhorts Timothy:

> *"Watch your life and doctrine closely. Persevere in them, because if you do, you will save both yourself and your hearers."*
>
> *— 1 Timothy 4:16 (NIV)*

This is not simply personal advice—it is an eternal principle. What you believe, and how you live in light of that belief, determines where your soul will dwell. The path to salvation is not walked by crowds; it is walked by individuals who have heard the voice of the Shepherd and chosen to follow.

And so, dear friend, I urge you: Do not build your life on borrowed assumptions or religious tradition. Open the Scriptures. Hear what Jesus himself has said. Be honest with yourself. Be humble before God. Salvation is not hidden. It is not complicated. But it does require your whole life.

> *"We must pay more careful attention, therefore, to what we have heard, so that we do not drift away... How shall we escape if we ignore so great a salvation?"*
>
> *— Hebrews 2:1–3 (NIV)*

This salvation was not invented by men. It was first announced by the Lord—and confirmed by those who heard him. It is now entrusted to us, not as a relic to admire, but as a message to obey. So let us begin—not with opinion or commentary, but with Jesus. Let us listen to his voice. Let us follow his path.

Because when the question is, What must I do to be saved?—no other answer will do.

3

An advice worth your soul

WHAT MUST I DO TO BE SAVED?

Contextomy

"the practice of misquoting someone by shortening the quotation or by leaving out surrounding words or sentences that would place the quotation in context"

One of the perennial tragedies of human communication—and indeed, of human nature itself—is our tendency to seize upon fragments, to wrench words out of their living context, and thereby distort the message they were meant to carry. This is no less true, perhaps even more tragically so, when it comes to the Holy Scriptures. The message that once resounded through dusty Galilean roads, that echoed in the hearts of fishermen and farmers, has often been fragmented and scattered like broken pottery, each piece held up as though it were the whole.

By the early 21st century, it was widely reported that Christianity had splintered into over 33,000 denominations worldwide. In many cities, you could find multiple churches on the same street, each claiming fidelity to the one Gospel, yet often interpreting it in diverging—even contradictory—ways. Contrast this with the early ecclesial vision: one Church per city, a unified body bearing witness to the risen Jesus. What we witness now is a far cry from the days when Paul wrote to "the church in Corinth" or "the saints in Ephesus."

To add complexity to confusion, the proliferation of Bible translations—though a gift in many ways—has also, at times, become a commercial enterprise rather than a theological labor of love. And amid this maze of interpretations and doctrines, groups often gather not in humble pursuit of truth, but to defend what they have always believed, drawing lines in the sand with verses taken in isolation, used as ammunition rather than revelation.

This phenomenon—what some have called "contextomy"—is not merely an academic oversight; it is, at heart, a spiritual malaise. It is a failure to listen—not just to words on a page, but to the living voice of God behind them. We are tempted to treat Scripture like a vault of ready-made answers rather than a grand, unfolding story in which we are summoned to participate.

When we quarrel over isolated verses, torn from their narrative roots, without pausing to understand the world of the speaker or the heart of the listener, we do not defend truth—we trade in half-truths. Such debates often produce heat, but little light.

Let me offer a word of counsel, not from a scholar or a bishop, but from a servant girl—nameless and exiled—whose simple faith saw what the powerful could not. Her words, nestled in a narrative from 2 Kings 5:1-19, become a beacon of what true hearing and humble faith might look like.

Naaman, a commander of armies, a man of stature and influence, found himself stricken with leprosy. Though he had seen victory by the hand of God, that did not spare him from the deep ache of personal affliction. And it was not through royal decree or military strategy that hope came, but through the quiet suggestion of a young girl in service: "If only my master would see the prophet who is in Samaria! He would cure him of his leprosy."

What follows is a story of misplaced expectations and wounded pride, of a powerful man almost refusing healing because it came in a form too humble for his grandeur. Yet, as his servants wisely urged, "If the prophet had told you to do some great thing, would you not have done it?... Wash and be cleansed." And so he did, and he was.

Naaman's story is our story. We too seek great answers and dramatic interventions, yet the healing word often comes in humble form. The voice of God, even now, speaks through Scripture—not in isolated prooftexts but in the grand narrative that culminates in Jesus the Messiah. We are called not merely to read, but to enter that story, to live in its context, and to allow its message to cleanse and restore us.

So as we begin this journey, let us heed the wisdom of the servant girl. Let us approach the Word not as those looking to prove our own rightness, but as those who, like Naaman, are in need of healing—and who must learn to listen, even when the message comes from unexpected places.

We must come to terms with a deeply uncomfortable truth that Scripture bears witness to again and again: God, in His sovereignty, often works through all kinds of people—righteous or wicked, noble or unworthy—as instruments to accomplish His purposes. The fact that someone is used by God does not, in itself, imply divine approval or guarantee divine blessing. The story of Naaman, the Aramean commander, draws this into sharp relief.

Naaman was, in the eyes of his peers, a great man. Accomplished, valiant, victorious. His reputation preceded him. And yet, beneath the armor and accolades, his body was slowly betraying him—leprosy gnawed away at his flesh, and no amount of glory could silence the question that haunted him through the night: "What must I do to be healed?"

Now here's the remarkable irony—and it's the kind of irony Scripture is filled with when you look closely. The same battlefields on which Naaman had experienced triumph, through which God had given him victory, also became the setting for his encounter with the divine whisper of redemption. In God's providence, among the spoils of war came a captured servant girl—an unnamed Israelite child—who held the key to Naaman's healing. This was not merely about a skin condition. This was a moment poised to unveil God Himself.

Whether Naaman would find his healing—and more than that, whether he would come to know the living God—depended entirely on the condition of his heart. Would he humble himself? Would he lay aside the expectations that came with his rank and status? Would he be willing to listen not to a king or a general, but to a prophet from a foreign land?

When Naaman finally arrived in Israel, expecting pomp and a prophet who would theatrically summon the name of YHWH, he was greeted not by God, but by a man of God. And this man gave him no elaborate ritual. No mystical ceremony. Just a bafflingly simple instruction: "Go, wash yourself seven times in the Jordan, and your flesh will be restored, and you will be cleansed" (2 Kings 5:10).

Naaman's response? Offense. Disappointment. Rage. And yet, this reaction tells us more about the human heart than it does about Naaman himself. How often do we resist the very thing that can heal us, simply because it defies our expectations?

Now let us imagine for a moment what might have happened had Naaman fallen prey to the subtle and dangerous temptation of theological rationalization—what we might call "contextomy in practice." These are not wild hypotheticals, but the very sorts of inner arguments we often entertain when the Word of God cuts across our preferences:

1. "Surely, God simply wants me to wash in a river. Rivers are all His creation, after all. I'll return to Damascus and bathe in the Abana—it's cleaner, grander, and far more familiar."
2. "I don't need to physically wash. Clearly, this is a metaphor. If I believe in my heart that God can heal, that should be enough."
3. "I believe in the promise. But what if I don't make it to the Jordan before I die? God knows my heart. I'll go later—when it's more convenient."

Each of these responses, however pious they might sound, misses the central point: obedience. Not theoretical, not philosophical—but actual, tangible submission to God's revealed word.

Naaman was blessed with wise servants—individuals who didn't theologize, but simply said, in effect: "Master, stop overthinking. Just do what God has asked." And when Naaman obeyed—not as a general, but as a humbled man—he was made clean (2 Kings 5:14). His skin, yes. But more profoundly, his heart was changed. He returned to Elisha declaring: "Now I know that there is no God in all the world except in Israel" (v. 15).

And this, dear reader, brings us to a sobering echo of Naaman's story in the New Testament.

"Teacher, what must I do to inherit eternal life?" (Luke 10:25). A question posed not by a foreign commander, but by a scholar of the Law. He knew the right answers: "Love the Lord your God… and your neighbor as yourself." (v. 27). But—just like Naaman—he wanted to justify himself. "And who is my neighbor?" he asked, fishing for a loophole.

Jesus, with the wisdom of the kingdom, told him a story that must have stunned him. A priest and a Levite—those steeped in scripture—pass by a wounded man. And then a Samaritan, the outsider, the presumed heretic, stops to help (Luke 10:30–35). In the end, Jesus asks: "Which of these was a neighbor?" And when the expert in the Law answers, Jesus says, "Go and do likewise" (v. 37).

There it is again: not merely to know the truth, but to live it. Not to recite the right answer, but to embody it. Knowledge of Scripture without obedience to it is no righteousness at all. The priest, the Levite, the legal expert—perhaps they saw themselves as God's representatives. But only the Samaritan represented God, because he acted in love and mercy. He embodied the kingdom.

So the call to Naaman, to the legal scholar, and to us is the same: Stop justifying yourself. Lay down your conditions. Listen to the voice of God, even if it comes through unexpected servants. And then—go, and do likewise.

Naaman and the expert in the law—two men from vastly different walks of life, one a Gentile warrior, the other a Jewish scholar—were both faced with the same core challenge: to obey the word of God, not as they expected it, but as it was given. Both received an invitation—not to explain, debate, or theologize—but to step into the healing and life that come only through faithful obedience.

For Naaman, the path to healing required a fundamental shift. He had to relinquish his assumptions about how divine power ought to work. He had to set aside the rivers he knew, the logic he trusted, and the status he bore. Had he followed any of the "reasonable" alternatives he devised—any of the clever theological footnotes we saw earlier—he would have remained a leper. His healing came not because he finally understood the deeper meaning of the Jordan, nor because he was brave, nor because he "believed" in some abstract sense. His healing came because he trusted the word spoken by the prophet and acted accordingly.

And that, of course, is grace. Not a cheap sentimentalism, but the shocking reality that God chooses to extend His mercy to those who, by every earthly measure, are undeserving. As Jesus Himself declared in Nazareth, "And there were many in Israel with leprosy in the time of Elisha the prophet, yet not one of them was cleansed—only Naaman the Syrian" (Luke 4:27, NIV).

Naaman was an outsider, a military commander in a nation hostile to Israel. He was, in every sense, an enemy of the people of God. And yet, he is the one to whom God extended healing. This is grace: God choosing to act in mercy, not because of who we are, but because of who He is.

But—and here's the critical point—grace does not nullify obedience; it calls it forth. Naaman's healing was a gift, but it was a gift that had to be received in humility, not on his own terms, but on God's.

Why spend so much time with this Old Testament account? Because, as the apostle Paul reminds us in his letter to the Romans, "everything that was written in the past was written to teach us, so that through endurance and the encouragement of the Scriptures we might have hope" (Romans 15:4, NIV). The Law and the Prophets—what we call the Old Testament—were not mere history lessons. They are living testimonies, God-focused narratives through which we learn the shape of faithful living and the contours of divine grace.

The lesson here is not academic. It's not about acquiring a more refined theology. It's about learning to hear—and obey—the voice of God. As you walk through these pages, with Scripture open before you, let the message ring clearly: God is not asking for your interpretations, your clever arguments, your denominational traditions, or your sacrifices. He is asking for your obedience.

As Samuel told Saul, in one of the most sobering moments of Israel's history:

"To obey is better than sacrifice, and to heed is better than the fat of rams. For rebellion is like the sin of divination, and arrogance like the evil of idolatry. Because you have rejected the word of the LORD, he has rejected you as king" (1 Samuel 15:22–23, NIV).

And again, "To do what is right and just is more acceptable to the LORD than sacrifice" (Proverbs 21:3, NIV).

Let me offer you one piece of counsel, as one walking this road beside you: be willing to set aside what you've always known. Let go of the comfort of inherited assumptions. Become like Naaman—willing to lay down pride, willing to admit you do not know, willing to receive instruction from unexpected places.

And above all, beware the danger of contextomy. When we strip God's words from their context to serve our own purposes, we do not find healing—we remain unchanged. The real question that echoes through Scripture is not simply, "What do I believe?" but "What must I do, Lord?"—and the only right response is faithful action in the direction of God's voice.

You do not gain anything by being "right" in the eyes of your tradition or community. You gain everything by doing what is right in the sight of God. And that is the path we now pursue together.

4

Who is this Jesus?

What must I do to be saved?

It's a question that echoes through the ages—a question that stirs the hearts of seekers and saints alike. Indeed, it's one of those rare questions that feels at once profoundly personal and urgently universal. And yet, despite its simplicity, the variety of answers one might encounter—across churches, traditions, and interpretations—can be overwhelming.

But as the writer of Hebrews reminds us, "Jesus the Messiah is the same yesterday and today and forever" (Hebrews 13:8). That is to say, the Jesus we meet in the Gospels is not a distant figure of a bygone era. He is present and active, speaking still. His words, his actions, his invitations—they are not locked in history but reverberate into our present.

And so, if we are to answer this vital question—"What must I do to be saved?"—we must begin where all Christian inquiry must begin: with Jesus himself. Not simply with our systems, not even with our theologies as such, but with Jesus—his own teachings, his own definition of the life he came to give.

Often, this question arises in a slightly different form: "What must I do to inherit eternal life?" This too is a deeply biblical phrasing, one that appears multiple times in the Gospel accounts. And yet, for many modern minds, the term "eternal life" can feel elusive—something distant, almost otherworldly. But Jesus, in what might be the most precise definition he gives, makes it startlingly clear. "Now this is eternal life: that they may know you, the only true God, and Jesus the Messiah, whom you have sent" (John 17:3).

In this one sentence, Jesus reframes salvation not as a future rescue mission, but as a relational reality. Eternal life is not merely about what happens after death; it is about knowing God now, through Jesus. To be saved, in the truest sense, is to be swept up into the intimate relationship that Jesus himself shares with the Father—a relationship marked by trust, obedience, and love.

So, our question—"What must I do to be saved?"—is not a matter of ticking religious boxes or subscribing to abstract beliefs. It is, at its heart, a matter of relationship: knowing God as Father, and Jesus as the one he has sent. To seek salvation, then, is to step into that relationship, to walk the path Jesus himself walked, and to discover along the way that eternal life is not only our future hope but our present reality in him.

Who is Jesus?

It's the question on which everything turns. Not merely a doctrinal curiosity or theological abstraction, but the very hinge upon which the entire Christian vision of salvation, of eternal life, of the renewal of all things, depends.

And yet, for all its weight and wonder, the Church has too often stumbled into confusion—not because the Scriptures are unclear, but because, like the Pharisees of old, we have not been content to receive what God has plainly revealed. We have, instead, tried to climb up by other means, spinning elaborate theologies that venture beyond what is written, rather than attending with humility to the story God has told.

Let us begin with what is given. The name Jesus—a Greek form of Yeshua, or Joshua—means "The Lord saves." Already in his name, we hear the echo of Israel's hope and the mission entrusted to him by the Father. But his birth fulfilled something even more ancient—a promise embedded in the prophetic imagination of Israel. As Isaiah declared, "The virgin will conceive and give birth to a son, and they will call him Immanuel—which means, God with us" (Isaiah 7:14; cf. Matthew 1:23).

That name, Immanuel, is not simply a title on a birth announcement. It is a claim—staggering in its implications—that in Jesus, the presence of Israel's God had come to dwell with his people. But does this mean that Jesus is, in some simple or abstract sense, "God"? For centuries, much ink has been spilled over that question. And sadly, much of it has served more to divide than to illuminate. In fact, when we take our eyes off the story—the story that the Scriptures are telling—we too easily reduce Jesus to a proposition to be dissected, rather than the person in whom God has acted decisively and definitively for the world's salvation.

The Scriptures do not invite us into speculative philosophy about the nature of God and Christ. They summon us to faith in the one whom God has sent.

What then must we believe, if we are to begin the journey into eternal life? The answer is both profound and beautifully simple: Jesus is the Christ, the Son of the living God.

That is the confession heaven itself affirms. At his birth, the angel announced, "The holy one to be born will be called the Son of God" (Luke 1:35). At his baptism and again at the Transfiguration, the voice of God broke through the veil of heaven, declaring, "This is my Son, whom I love; with him I am well pleased" (Matthew 3:17; 17:5).

And when Jesus asked his disciples that haunting question—"Who do you say I am?"—it was not a moment for theological guesswork. It was a moment of divine revelation. Peter, speaking not from his own insight but from a gift of the Father, replied, "You are the Christ, the Son of the living God" (Matthew 16:16). To which Jesus responded, "Blessed are you, Simon son of Jonah, for this was not revealed to you by flesh and blood, but by my Father in heaven" (Matthew 16:17).

This confession stands at the very foundation of the Christian faith. Not merely that Jesus said wise things. Not merely that he performed signs. But that in him, the long-awaited Messiah had come—the true Son, who bears the name and image of Israel's God, who reveals the Father's heart, and who invites us into a life made new.

To begin the journey of eternal life, then, is not to assent to a formula. It is to behold Jesus, trust what the Father has said about him, and follow him into the life he alone can give.

WHAT MUST I DO TO BE SAVED?

Timeline of Christ's Life

Christ's birth	winter 5/4 B.C.
Herod the Great's death	March/April 4 BC.
Prefects began to rule over Judea, Samaria	AD. 6
Christ at the temple when twelve	Passover, April 29, 9
Caiaphas became high priest	AD. 18
Pilate arrived in Judea	AD. 26
Commencement of John the Baptist's ministry	AD. 29
Commencement of Christ's ministry	summer/autumn AD. 29
Christ's first Passover (John 2:13)	April 7, 30
John the Baptist imprisoned	AD. 30 or 31
Christ's second Passover	April 25. 31
John the Baptist's death	AD. 31 or 32
Christ at the Feast of Tabernacles (John 5:1)	October 21 -28. 31
Christ's third Passover (John 6:4)	April 13/14. 32
Christ at Feast of Tabernacles (John 7:2. 10)	September 10-17. 32
Christ at Feast of Dedication (John 10:22-39)	December 18. 32
Christ's final week .	March 28 - April 5. 33
Arrived at Bethany	Saturday. March 28
Crowds at Bethany	Sunday. March 29
Triumphal entry	Monday. March 30
Cursed fig tree and cleansed temple	Tuesday. March 31
Temple controversy and Olivet discourse Christ's	Wednesday. April 1
Passover, betrayed, arrested & tried	Thursday. April 2
Christ tried and crucified	Friday. April 3
Christ laid in the tomb	Saturday. April 4
Christ resurrected	Sunday, April 5
Christ's ascension (Acts 1)	Thursday. May 14, 33
Day of Pentecost (Acts 2)	Sunday, May 24, 33

The Testimony of God and the Revelation of His Son

We are, all of us, shaped by stories—stories we inherit, stories we live by, stories we trust. But there is one story that stands above the rest, because it is not merely man's account of the divine, but God's own testimony concerning his Son. As the apostle John puts it with startling clarity: "We accept human testimony, but God's testimony is greater because it is the testimony of God, which he has given about his Son. Whoever believes in the Son of God accepts this testimony. Whoever does not believe God has made him out to be a liar..." (1 John 5:9–10).

Before the birth of a man called Jesus, there was God	After the birth of Jesus, there was God and there was a man called Jesus, a man in whom the spirit of God dwelt without measure. A man who was the presence of God among people.	After his resurrection, there is God and there is the Christ, the son of God, not flesh and blood.

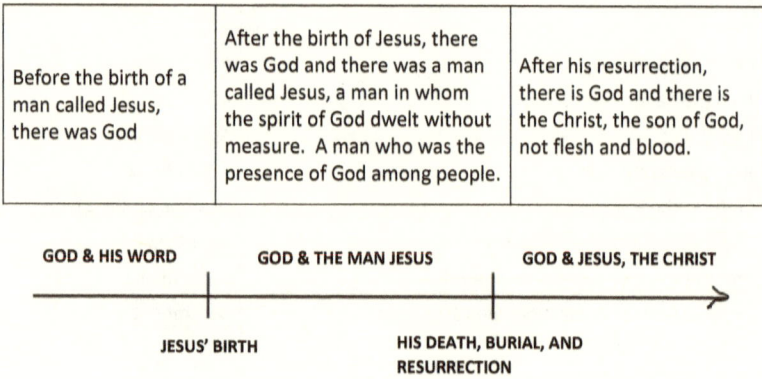

Jesus as the presence of God was with the Israelites because of the ark of God, in which the spirit of God wholly resided, so the presence of God was here as his spirit wholly dwelled in flesh and blood, in Jesus on earth.

The shape of that testimony is simple, yet staggeringly profound: "God has given us eternal life, and this life is in his Son" (1 John 5:11). In other words, the life God intends for his world—renewed, restored, eternal—is found in the person of Jesus the Messiah. The fullness of life, the presence of God, the rescue of creation—it is all bound up in him.

But who is he?

In Philippians 2:5–11, Paul draws us into the great paradox of the gospel: that Jesus, though sharing the very form and identity of God, "did not consider equality with God something to be grasped". Instead, he humbled himself—taking the form of a servant, embracing the frailty of human flesh, submitting even to death on a cross. This, Paul insists, is not a denial of his divine status but the very expression of it. This is what it looks like when the living God reveals himself in power—not by dominating, but by self-giving love.

The letter to the Hebrews adds another dimension: "Although he was a son, he learned obedience through what he suffered" (Hebrews 5:8). Here again, the humanity of Jesus is not a mask or illusion, but real and full. He shared in our weaknesses. He faced our temptations. He walked our road—not above it, but through it.

So we do not begin with abstract metaphysics or speculative theology. We begin with the story: the Word became flesh. Jesus is the Son of the living God, the one in whom the fullness of God came to dwell—not as a vague spiritual presence, but as a man born of a woman, walking the dusty roads of Galilee. In him, the invisible God became visible. In him, the eternal Word became touchable. He is not God masquerading as man, nor a man climbing toward divinity. He is the Son—eternally in relation to the Father, now revealed in time and space, fully human, fully obedient, and fully filled with the presence of God.

This is no mere theological nuance. It is the heartbeat of Christian faith. For just as the ark once carried the presence of God among the Israelites, now in Jesus the living presence of God has come to dwell among his people in a far deeper, more personal way. To see him is to see the Father—not because he is the Father, but because he is the true and faithful image, the exact imprint of God's being (Hebrews 1:3).

Before he was born, he was mystery. The Word, with God and as God, beyond all human comprehension. But in the fullness of time, the Word became flesh (John 1:14). He did not descend as a fully-formed divine being in disguise. He was born—flesh and blood, vulnerable, human—yet in him, the fullness of deity dwelt.

To acknowledge Jesus as the Son of the living God, therefore, is not merely to agree with a statement. It is to receive the testimony of God himself. It is to recognize that in Jesus, God has made himself known—not in abstract theory, but in a crucified and risen man, who embodies the divine character in full.

And this, quite simply, is where the road to salvation begins: with the confession that Jesus is the Christ, the Son of the living God. In him, eternal life is not a distant hope, but a present reality—because in him, God has drawn near.

Repentance and the Nearness of God's Kingdom

When Jesus stepped into the waters of the Jordan to be baptized by John, he was not merely performing a symbolic gesture. He was identifying himself with the people he had come to rescue. He was saying "yes" to God's call, not only in principle, but in practice—

submitting himself to the mission that would lead through the cross to resurrection and new creation.

And from that moment, his message was unmistakably clear: "Repent, for the kingdom of heaven is at hand" (Matthew 4:17).

But what does that mean? Repent—from what? And why?

These are not merely religious questions, as though repentance were one more item on a checklist of personal piety. No, they are deeply human questions. To ask them is to stand at the crossroads of God's story and your own. For if Jesus has come to bring God's kingdom—God's sovereign, healing, restoring rule—then it confronts us with the undeniable truth: something in us, in our world, and in the systems we've built is out of joint. Something must change.

To repent is not simply to feel bad or guilty. It is to turn around. To face a new direction. It is to reorient your life around a new reality: that God's kingdom is breaking in, and that your old ways—ways of self-protection, self-deception, injustice, and pride—do not fit the shape of the world God is making.

Jesus himself makes this purpose explicit when he stands in the synagogue and reads from the scroll of Isaiah:

"The Spirit of the Lord is upon me, because he has anointed me to proclaim good news to the poor. He has sent me to proclaim liberty to the captives and recovery of sight to the blind, to set the oppressed free, to proclaim the year of the Lord's favor" (Luke 4:18–19).

This is not the language of mere inward change. This is the language of liberation. Of re-creation. Of a radical undoing and remaking of lives under the reign of God's justice and mercy. Repentance, then, is not about wallowing in shame; it is about throwing off the chains that keep us blind, imprisoned, and bowed low under the weight of brokenness—both ours and the world's.

And yet, let us not romanticize it. Repentance is hard. It is a wrestling with ourselves, with our illusions, with the comfortable falsehoods we've told ourselves about what really matters. It demands honesty—a deep, unflinching gaze into the mirror of God's righteousness. As John's baptism demonstrated, repentance is not vague remorse. It is concrete. It involves justice, generosity, humility, and a reckoning with how we treat our neighbors, how we hold our possessions, and how we steward the short lives we've been given.

That's why the people who came to John didn't leave unchanged. They were challenged to look squarely at their character, their actions, and their responsibilities. They were being prepared—not merely for religious experience, but for a kingdom that would demand their whole selves.

Many live lives marked by quiet despair, habits of dishonesty, cycles of pain, and a haunting sense that something has been lost. But repentance opens the door to a new possibility—a life lived in tune with the grace, truth, and purpose of God's coming reign. It is not the end, but the beginning of salvation's path.

And so, Jesus' call rings out still: "Repent, for the kingdom of heaven has drawn near." To heed that call is not to embrace fear, but to

WHAT MUST I DO TO BE SAVED?

embrace freedom. It is to be invited into a story bigger than our failures—and to find ourselves remade in the light of God's future.

Chronology of Jesus' ministry

EVENT	PLACE	TIME	MATTHEW	MARK	LUKE	JOHN
From Beginning to Final Week:						
Jesus is baptized	Jordan River	c. A.D.	3:13-17	1:9-11	3:21-23	1:29-39
Jesus is tempted by Satan	Wilderness	26(29)	4:1-11	1:12-13	4:1-13	
Jesus performs His first miracle	Cana					2:1-11
Jesus and Nicodemus converse	Judea	27(30)				3:1-21
Jesus talks to the Samaritan woman	Samaria					4:5-42
Jesus heals a nobleman's son	Cana					4:46-54
The people of Jesus' hometown try to kill Him	Nazareth				4:16-31	
Four fishermen become Jesus' followers	Sea of Galilee		4:18-22	1:16-20	5:1-11	
Jesus heals Peter's mother-in-law	Capernaum		8:14-17	1:29-34	4:38-41	
Jesus begins His first preaching trip through Galilee	Galilee		4:23-25	1:35-39	4:42-44	
Matthew decides to follow Jesus	Capernaum		9:9-13	2:13-17	5:27-32	
Jesus chooses the Twelve		28(31)		3:13-19	6:12-15	
Jesus preaches the "Sermon on the Mount"			5:1-7:29		6:20-49	
A sinful woman anoints Jesus	Capernaum				7:36-50	
Jesus travels again through Galilee					8:1-3	
Jesus tells parables about the kingdom			13:1-52	4:1-34	8:4-18	
Jesus quiets the storm	Sea of Galilee		8:23-27	4:35-41	8:22-25	
Jairus's daughter is brought back to life by Jesus	Capernaum		9:18-26	5:21-43	8:40-56	
Jesus sends the Twelve out to preach and heal			9:35-11:1	6:6-13	9:1-6	
John the Baptist is killed by Herod	Machaerus		14:1-12	6:14-29	9:7-9	
Jesus feeds 5,000 people	Near Bethsaida	Spring 29(32)	14:13-21	6:30-34	9:10-17	6:1-14
Jesus walks on water			14:22, 23	6:45-52		6:16-21
Jesus feeds 4,000 people		Later in the year	15:32-39	8:1-9		
Peter says that Jesus is the Son of God			16:13-20	8:27-30	9:18-21	
Jesus tells His disciples He is going to die soon	Caesarea Philippi		16:21-26	8:31-37	9:22-25	
Jesus is transfigured			17:1-3	9:2-13	9:28-36	
Jesus pays His temple tax	Capernaum		17:24-27			
Jesus attends the Feast of Tabernacles	Jerusalem	October 29(32)				7:11-52
Jesus heals a man who was born blind	Jerusalem	Later in the year				9:1-41
Jesus visits Mary and Martha	Bethany				10:38-42	
Jesus raises Lazarus from the dead	Bethany	Winter 29(32)				11:1-44
Jesus begins His last trip to Jerusalem		30(33)			17:11	
Jesus blesses the little children	Across the Jordan		19:13-16	10:13-16	18:15-17	
Jesus talks to the rich young man	Across the Jordan		19:16-30	10:17-31	18:18-30	
Jesus again tells about His death and resurrection	Near the Jordan		20:17-19	10:32-34	18:31-34	
Jesus heals blind Bartimaeus	Jericho		20:29-34	10:46-52	18:35-43	
Jesus talks to Zacchaeus	Jericho				19:1-10	
Jesus returns to Bethany to visit Mary and Martha	Bethany	Friday				11:55-12:1

Chronology of Jesus' ministry (cont'd)

EVENT	PLACE	TIME	MATTHEW	MARK	LUKE	JOHN
The Final Week:						
Jesus enters Jerusalem on a donkey	Jerusalem	Sunday	21:1-17	11:1-11	19:29-44	
Jesus curses the fig tree	Jerusalem	Monday	21:18-19	11:12-14		
Jesus cleanses the temple	Jerusalem	Monday	21:12-13	11:15-18	19:45-46	
Jesus' authority is questioned	Jerusalem	Tuesday	21:23-22:14	11:27-12:12	20:1-19	
Jesus teaches in the temple	Jerusalem	Tuesday	22:41-46	12:35-37	20:41-44	
Mary anoints Jesus	Jerusalem	Tuesday	26:6-13	14:3-9		12:2-8
There is a plot to betray Jesus	Jerusalem	Wednesday(?)	26:14-16	14:10-11	22:3-6	
Jesus and His disciples eat Last Supper	Jerusalem	Thursday	26:17-25	14:12-21	22:7-30	13:1-30
Jesus gives His farewell discourse	Jerusalem	Thursday				14-16
Jesus prays in Gethsemane	Jerusalem	Thursday	26:30-36	14:26-42	22:39-46	18:1
Jesus is arrested and is tried by the Sanhedrin	Jerusalem	Friday	26:47-27:1	14:43-15:1	22:47-71	18:2-27
Jesus is tried by Pilate	Jerusalem	Friday	27:2-26	15:1-15	23:1-25	18:28-19:16
Jesus is crucified	Jerusalem	Friday	27:31-56	15:20-46	23:26-49	19:16-30
Jesus is buried	Jerusalem	Friday-Sunday	27:57-66	15:42-47	23:50-56	19:31-42
After the Resurrection:						
The tomb is seen to be empty	Jerusalem	Sunday	28:1-10	16:1-8	24:1-12	20:1-10
Mary Magdalene sees Jesus in the garden	Jerusalem	Sunday		16:9-11		20:11-18
Jesus appears to the two going to Emmaus		Sunday		16:12-13	24:13-35	
Jesus appears to ten disciples	Jerusalem	Sunday			24:36-43	20:19-25
Jesus appears to the Eleven	Jerusalem	One week later		16:14		20:26-31
Jesus talks with some of His disciples	Sea of Galilee					21:1-25
Jesus returns to His Father in heaven	Mt. of Olives	Forty days later	28:16-20	16:19-20	24:44-53	

The Call to Repent: God's Faithfulness and Our Turning

It all begins with a promise. Long before Jesus stepped onto the scene, God had spoken through the prophet Jeremiah, assuring his people that he had not abandoned his creation. "I will be their God, and they shall be my people... I will put my law within them, and I will write it on their hearts" (Jeremiah 31:33). This was not a vague spiritual comfort. It was a covenantal commitment—a pledge from the Creator to set the world right, to care for what he had made, and to heal the hearts of his wayward people.

It is within that divine promise that Jesus arrives—not as a detached spiritual guru, but as the embodiment of God's faithfulness, the one in whom God's rescue mission begins to take human form.

And yet, with Jesus' arrival comes a jarring announcement: "Repent, for the kingdom of heaven is at hand" (Matthew 4:17). He does not begin with warm reassurance. He begins with a challenge. A confrontation. A call to turn around.

Why?

Because the arrival of God's kingdom is not simply a religious idea—it is a reality that exposes the deep fractures in our lives. To repent is to acknowledge that something has gone terribly wrong. That we've lived out of step with the very design of our humanity. That the habits and systems we've constructed—often self-serving, often indifferent to justice and mercy—cannot coexist with the rule of the living God.

So, before we ask what we must repent of, we must first ask why.

And the answer, perhaps surprisingly, is not guilt—but grace.

We repent not simply because we are bad and need fixing, but because the kingdom is coming, and we have the opportunity to be part of it. We repent because God's new world is breaking in, and the lives we have been living are too small, too broken, too misaligned with God's purposes to carry forward into that new creation.

Jesus' call to repent is not the angry demand of a distant judge—it is the urgent invitation of the world's rightful King, calling us to reorient our lives around his rule of justice, mercy, and truth. To repent is to say yes to the new thing God is doing. It is to come into alignment with his heart, to receive his mercy, and to become the kind of people through whom his kingdom life can flow.

In short, we must repent because God is faithful. Because God has come near. Because God has not given up on his world—or on us. And if we are to be part of what he is doing, then something in us must change.

The Kingdom of God

The Coming Kingdom and the Call to Repent

"Repent, for the kingdom of God is at hand." These were not just the opening words of Jesus' public ministry—they were the thunderclap signaling that something decisive, something long-promised and long-awaited, was breaking into history.

Why the call to repentance? Because the kingdom of God was not merely a religious metaphor or a private spiritual experience. It was, and remains, a reality charged with consequence—a new reign, a new creation, a new way of being human, all under the rule of Israel's God.

To grasp the weight of Jesus' words, we must see them as the climax of a story already in motion. The prophet Daniel, speaking nearly five centuries before Jesus, had interpreted a dream that haunted the mind of a Babylonian king—a dream not of personal fortune, but of world empires and divine sovereignty. In the dream, the king saw a towering statue, dazzling and terrifying, composed of various metals: gold, silver, bronze, iron, and clay (Daniel 2:31–33). Each material symbolized a successive kingdom—first Babylon, then the Medo-Persian empire, followed by the Greeks, and finally the Roman empire.

And then—unexpected, unmade by human hands—a rock struck the feet of the statue. It shattered the whole edifice. All the empires, once so mighty, crumbled to dust and were swept away like chaff. And that stone? It grew into a mountain that filled the whole earth

(Daniel 2:34–35). "In the time of those kings, the God of heaven will set up a kingdom that will never be destroyed" (Daniel 2:44).

This is no mere dream—it is a divine unveiling, a prophetic lens through which we can see history's movement toward God's intended goal. And so when Jesus stands, centuries later, in the very world ruled by Rome, and announces that the kingdom of God is near, he is not beginning a new story—he is bringing God's ancient promises to their long-awaited fulfillment.

This kingdom, however, is unlike any other. It is not built by military might or political ambition. It does not advance through conquest or coercion. It is a kingdom not cut by human hands but born of God himself—rooted in righteousness, animated by mercy, inaugurated through self-giving love.

That's why repentance is not an optional spiritual exercise—it is the doorway into this new world. To enter the kingdom, we must lay down the patterns of the old. The kingdoms of this world are built on pride, fear, violence, and self-rule. But the kingdom of God calls for a different kind of sovereignty—God's sovereignty over our lives, our loyalties, our loves.

And so Jesus' call to repentance is not harsh—it is hopeful. He invites us to realign our lives with the reign of God, to leave behind the false securities of earthly empires and the brokenness of our own waywardness. The world's kingdoms come and go, but the kingdom of God is an everlasting kingdom—a mountain that fills the earth.

To repent is to turn from the shadows and step into that kingdom's light.

Views on the dream Daniel interpreted.

NEBUCHADENEZZAR'S DREAM STATUE (Dan 2)	DANIEL'S VISION OF BEASTS (Dan 7)	POSITION #1	POSITION #2	POSITION #3
HEAD GOLD	Lion with eagle wings	BABYLON	BABYLON	Nebuchadnezzer (2:38)
CHEST SILVER	Bear	MEDIA	MEDO-PERSIA	MEDIA Contemporaneous to Nebuchadnezzar's successors
	3 Ribs in mouth	Darius the Mede		
TORSO BRONZE	Leopard with	PERSIA	GREEK	PERSIA
	4 wings and 4 heads	First 4 Persian kings or 4 directions	4 generals who divide up Alexander's Empire	First 4 kings of Persia (Dan 11:2)
LEGS IRON, FEET IRON, and POTTERY	Unnamed Beast	GREECE	ROMAN	GREECE
	10 horns	10 horns Selected Kings Little horn – Antichus IV, Epiphanes	3 options: Past fulfillment Future Fulfillment in extended empire Future Fulfillment in reconstituted empire	10 horns – 10 sovereign states that had grown out of Alexander's empire by the 2nd B.C.

What, then, is the nature of this kingdom to which Jesus calls us—a kingdom so vital that it demands a radical reorientation of life itself?

In the empires and nations of the world, one's experience of life is so often shaped by status, tribe, ethnicity, or class. The prevailing powers and principalities have always rendered justice uneven, peace fragile, and flourishing selective. Yet every rule reveals its character through the kind of life it generates. So too with the kingdom of God: the nature of this kingdom is disclosed not in abstract doctrine but in the concrete life Jesus both proclaimed and embodied.

From the very outset of the gospel narrative, we see that Jesus did not inaugurate this kingdom in a vacuum. Rather, he took up the message first sounded by John the Baptist—a call to repentance, to turn from the old ways of exile and despair and toward the promise of God's coming reign. This was not a vague moral exhortation. It was the urgent announcement that Israel's long-awaited hope was breaking into history. The reign of God, long prophesied, was arriving. And Jesus, stepping into public ministry at around the age of thirty, takes up this same message:

> *"Jesus went throughout Galilee, teaching in their synagogues, preaching the good news of the kingdom, and healing every disease and sickness among the people."* (Matthew 4:23)

This, then, was the agenda of the kingdom: healing, restoration, liberation—a dramatic inbreaking of God's rule into the broken fabric of the world.

And this kingdom, Jesus insists, is no late innovation. It is the telos toward which the Law and the Prophets pointed, the culmination of Israel's long and often troubled story. As he declares:

> *"From the days of John the Baptist until now, the kingdom of heaven has been forcefully advancing, and forceful men lay hold of it. For all the Prophets and the Law prophesied until John."* (Matthew 11:12–13)

Here we stand at the intersection of two ages—the old order, groaning under the weight of injustice, and the new age, which arrives not with the sword but with the word, not with domination but with mercy. Those who responded to John's baptism were aligning themselves with this new reality. They recognized in John's call the voice of the one crying in the wilderness: "Prepare the way for the Lord."

But not all responded. As Luke tells us:

> "The Pharisees and the experts in the law rejected God's purpose for themselves, because they had not been baptized by John." (Luke 7:30)

To reject John's baptism was to reject the eschatological turn—the moment when God's kingdom was emerging in real time, calling all to repentance and allegiance to the Messiah.

Jesus made no illusion that this kingdom would be universally embraced. On the contrary, he spoke of a dramatic reversal that would confound expectations:

> "There will be weeping there and gnashing of teeth, when you see Abraham, Isaac and Jacob and all the prophets in the kingdom of God, but you yourselves thrown out. People will come from east and west and north and south and will take their places at the feast in the kingdom of God." (Luke 13:28–29)

This is not mere poetry; it is the prophetic unveiling of a kingdom rooted not only in the future but also in the past and deeply connected to Israel's patriarchs and prophets. This feast, then, is not for the privileged or the presumed, but for the faithful and the humble—those who discern in Jesus the true shape of Israel's vocation and God's redemptive plan.

Jesus also speaks of this kingdom as something prepared "since the creation of the world" (Matthew 25:34). This is not a political program but a divine vocation for humanity itself. And he illustrates its nature with stories drawn from everyday life. In one such parable, he says:

> *"The kingdom of heaven is like a man who sowed good seed in his field..." (Matthew 13:24–29)*

The image is striking. Jesus, the true sower, scatters good seed across the world. But the field is contested territory; there are other forces at work—sowers of weeds, agents of confusion and counterfeit. And yet, this is not a call to violent purging or triumphalist purity. God's judgment is patient, just, and reserved for the right time. As Jesus later explains (Matthew 13:36–43), the wheat and the weeds must grow together until the harvest, when the Son of Man will send his angels to gather the sons of the kingdom.

Here lies one of the great paradoxes of the kingdom: it arrives in weakness, it grows in secret, and it calls forth faith. Jesus' kingdom is not about domination but transformation; not about separation from the world but about renewal from within it.

So we return to our question: What is this kingdom for which we are called to reorder our lives?

It is the long-promised reign of Israel's God breaking into the present through the life, death, and resurrection of Jesus the Messiah. It is a kingdom that draws its citizens not by force but by grace. It is sown through the preaching of the good news and yields its harvest in those who respond with faith and repentance. And its citizens are those who, like Abraham, Isaac, and Jacob, live by the promise of God, trusting that the one who sows in tears will indeed reap with joy.

As Jesus journeyed through Jericho, speaking yet again of the kingdom of God, he revealed something central—not just about the message he proclaimed, but about the mission he embodied. In Luke 19:10, we hear the Messiah himself declare, "For the Son of Man came to seek and to save what was lost." This is not an abstract statement of spiritual recovery; it is the climax of Israel's story, where God himself, in and through Jesus, is returning to rescue his wayward people and to reconstitute them as the renewed people of God—the children of the kingdom.

This gathering of the lost was not about boundary-markers like race, geography, or ritual purity, but about hearts turned back to God. Those who responded to Jesus' invitation found themselves, sometimes to their own astonishment, already standing within the domain of God's rule. For the kingdom Jesus proclaimed was not a political coup or the rise of a new geopolitical regime. It was, as he declared in Luke 17:20–21, a reality that defied human expectations:

> "The kingdom of God does not come with your careful observation, nor will people say, 'Here it is,' or 'There it is,' because the kingdom of God is within you."

Here is the paradox: the kingdom is both already present and still to come; hidden and yet decisive; unseen by the unrepentant, but unmistakable to those with eyes of faith. It is not something one can pinpoint on a map, nor is it a future dream detached from the present. Rather, it is the reign of God breaking into the world through the ministry of Jesus and continuing through those who bear his life.

But what, then, does it mean to enter this kingdom?

Jesus gives a disturbing yet clarifying answer in the Gospels. In both Mark and Matthew, he uses vivid imagery to underline the radical nature of discipleship:

> *"If your hand causes you to sin, cut it off... it is better for you to enter life maimed than with two hands to go into hell."* (Mark 9:43–47)

> *"If your eye causes you to sin, gouge it out... it is better for you to enter life with one eye than to have two eyes and be thrown into the fire of hell."* (Matthew 18:8–9)

These are not instructions for literal mutilation, but rather shocking metaphors that wake us up to the cost of discipleship and the weightiness of God's call. Life in God's kingdom demands a fierce kind of integrity, a willingness to part with whatever hinders our fidelity to the King. And notice what Jesus equates here: "entering life" is synonymous with "entering the kingdom." This kingdom is not simply a realm we inhabit; it is a life we are summoned into, a life shaped by holiness, wholeness, and radical obedience.

This point is driven home in the familiar and unsettling story of the rich young man (Matthew 19:16–24). The question he poses—"What good thing must I do to get eternal life?"—was, in many ways, the burning question of every faithful Jew in Jesus' time. The answer Jesus gives first affirms the enduring significance of God's commandments. But then he presses further. The call is not merely to moral observance, but to sacrificial allegiance:

> *"If you want to be perfect, go, sell your possessions and give to the poor... Then come, follow me."*

Here we see that salvation is not a transaction but a transformation. Eternal life, the kingdom of God, following Jesus—these are not separate concepts, but one and the same reality viewed from different angles. The man walks away, not because the offer is unclear, but because the cost is too great. And Jesus concludes with words that would have shocked his disciples:

> *"It is hard for a rich man to enter the kingdom of heaven... it is easier for a camel to go through the eye of a needle than for a rich man to enter the kingdom of God."*

In this single episode, we find Jesus redefining kingdom citizenship in stark terms: it is not inherited, bought, or achieved by social status. It is entered through surrender, through the letting go of all that competes with God's reign in our lives.

So, what have we seen so far?

We have traced the arc of the kingdom of God—from its deep roots with Abraham and the patriarchs, to its prophetic announcement through John, to its dramatic realization in the ministry of Jesus. We have seen that the kingdom is not simply a future event or a heavenly destination, but a life—the life of God shared with humanity. It is the gift of salvation, the fruit of obedience, and the birthright of those who respond to the good news of the Messiah.

And crucially, it is this good news—this announcement that Israel's God is becoming King in and through Jesus—that produces the sons and daughters of the kingdom. They are not defined by bloodline or status, but by repentance, faith, and fidelity to the King who gave himself for them.

If, as the prophets declared, the living God would one day establish his kingdom on earth, we must ask: When would that happen, and what would it look like when it did?

This was not a new question. It burned within the hearts of Israel's faithful, echoed through their prayers and longings. And it was asked quite directly of Jesus himself. The Pharisees, ever watchful for signs and portents, once pressed him: "When will the kingdom of God come?" (Luke 17:20). Jesus' reply dismantled their assumptions and ours:

> *"The kingdom of God does not come with your careful observation, nor will people say, 'Here it is,' or 'There it is,' because the kingdom of God is within you." (Luke 17:20–21)*

This is no denial of the kingdom's arrival; far from it. Rather, it is a redefinition of how God's kingdom operates. It is not a spectacle. It does not arrive with fanfare, tanks, or coronation. It does not conform to earthly notions of power and control. Instead, it begins like a seed sown in the hidden soil of the human heart—its growth mysterious, its effects transformative. This kingdom is not about territory, but about allegiance. It is not marked by borders, but by obedience. And its presence is known through the lives of those who have surrendered themselves to God's reign.

But then, if the kingdom is already here—"within you," as Jesus says—why does he also proclaim, "Repent, for the kingdom of God is at hand"? The answer lies in what Jesus actually brings.

In one dramatic moment, the religious leaders accuse Jesus of consorting with dark powers when he casts out demons. Jesus' response is as brilliant as it is revelatory:

> "If I drive out demons by the Spirit of God, then the kingdom of God has come upon you." (Matthew 12:28)

Here we see it plainly: the kingdom of God is not an abstract hope, but a present power. It has already come upon them—in the person of Jesus, in the authority he exercises, in the liberation he brings. Where Jesus is, the reign of God is breaking in. The world is being reclaimed, house by house, life by life, from the grip of the enemy. Jesus' authority is not borrowed; it is divine. His casting out of demons is not proof of sorcery, but of sovereignty.

He explains this further through parables—those deceptively simple stories that conceal profound truths. In one, he says:

> "The kingdom of God is like a man who scatters seed on the ground... the seed sprouts and grows, though he does not know how." (Mark 4:26–29)

And again:

> "It is like a mustard seed... the smallest of all seeds, yet when it grows it becomes the largest of all garden plants." (Mark 4:30–32)

The message is unmistakable: the kingdom begins small, quietly. It does not storm the gates of empire. It does not announce itself with fanfare. But it grows, inevitably and powerfully. First the stalk, then the head, then the full kernel in the head—until the time of harvest arrives. In other words, Jesus' preaching of the kingdom is not the end of the story, but its beginning. He is scattering seed, proclaiming the good news, and calling people into a new allegiance. The harvest—those who belong to God's renewed people—will emerge in time.

And who are these people?

They are those whom Jesus came to seek and to save (Luke 19:10). They are the ones called out—ekklesia in Greek, what we call the Church. Not a building, not a denomination, but a people gathered around a confession. For when Peter declares, "You are the Christ, the Son of the living God," Jesus replies:

> *"On this rock I will build my church, and the gates of Hades will not overcome it. I will give you the keys of the kingdom of heaven." (Matthew 16:15–19)*

This is no mere religious community. This is the kingdom community—the advance guard of God's new world. Built not on bloodlines, nor on moral achievement, but on the unshakable truth that Jesus is the Messiah, the Son of the living God. Where this confession is proclaimed, and where lives are reshaped in its light, there the kingdom is present.

So then, when will the kingdom come?

It has already come—in Jesus. It is still coming—in and through the Church. And it will one day come in fullness, when Christ returns to set the world finally to rights. But even now, the signs are visible—not to those who watch the skies for signs, but to those who see the poor lifted up, the broken healed, the lost brought home, and lives reordered around the crucified and risen King.

This is the kingdom of God on earth as it is in heaven.

It is no small thing to say that this moment in Caesarea Philippi—where Peter confesses Jesus as "the Christ, the Son of the living God" (Matthew 16:16)—stands as one of the pivotal declarations in the Gospel narrative. Yet it is also one of the most frequently misread and misapplied.

Some have taken Jesus' response to Peter as a justification for the institutional hierarchy of the Church—arguing that Peter, as the so-called "rock," was elevated as the foundation of the Church universal and therefore endowed with singular, even dynastic, authority. From this, the notion of papal succession was conceived. Others, in reaction, have flattened the entire passage, equating the Church itself with the Kingdom of God, as though the two were one and the same.

Both positions, however, misplace the emphasis.

Let us be clear: the heart of this moment is not Peter as a person, but the truth to which he bears witness. Jesus affirms this explicitly:

> "Blessed are you, Simon son of Jonah, for this was not revealed to you by man, but by my Father in heaven." (Matthew 16:17)

The foundation is not flesh and blood. It is not Peter's status. It is the divine revelation—the unveiling of Jesus as the Messiah, the Anointed One, the true Son of the living God. This is the bedrock upon which Jesus will build his community. Without this, there is no Church. Without this truth, there is no household of God, no citizenship in the Kingdom.

So what of the "keys of the kingdom"?

In the culture of Jesus' day, especially in Aramaic-speaking communities, to give someone the keys to a house meant something deeply specific: it meant entrusting them with delegated authority—much like assigning someone as the executor of a household in the master's absence. The keys were not the badge of exaltation, but of stewardship.

> *"I will give you the keys of the kingdom of heaven; whatever you bind on earth will be bound in heaven, and whatever you loose on earth will be loosed in heaven." (Matthew 16:19)*

This, then, is not a charter for ecclesiastical supremacy. It is a commissioning. Peter is being entrusted—just as Moses once was—not with dominion over the people, but with a task within God's kingdom: to announce, to discern, to act as a faithful steward of the kingdom message in Jesus' absence.

And indeed, we see Peter doing exactly this in the early chapters of Acts. He opens the doors of the kingdom to Jews at Pentecost, to Samaritans shortly after, and finally to Gentiles in the house of Cornelius. He does not stand over the Church as its monarch, but within it as its servant, announcing the implications of the risen Christ for all nations.

To confuse this role with a permanent office—especially one built around the accumulation of power—is to miss the entire ethos of the kingdom Jesus came to inaugurate.

Furthermore, we must not collapse the kingdom of God into the visible church. The Church—ekklesia, the called-out ones—is that segment of the kingdom visible on earth, the household gathered around the confession of Jesus as Lord. But the kingdom of God is broader, deeper, more mysterious. It is the reign of God breaking into history, and while the Church is called to embody that reign, it must never imagine itself as synonymous with it.

The danger is real. The Church, when it forgets its calling and confuses its mission, begins to demand outward obedience rather than inward transformation. It trades the joy of covenant relationship for the machinery of control. It lays burdens upon people that neither it nor their ancestors could bear (cf. Acts 15:10). It becomes, in essence, the very kind of institution that Jesus came to challenge: one defined by fear, hierarchy, and ritualized power, rather than by love, service, and truth.

Jesus did not come to found a religious organization built on regulations. He came to call a people whose hearts have been pierced by the truth of who he is. A people set free to obey—not through compulsion, but through love. A people built on the rock of divine revelation, shaped by grace, and ordered around the lordship of the crucified and risen King.

This is the household of God. This is the Church. And this is how the kingdom continues to come on earth as it is in heaven.

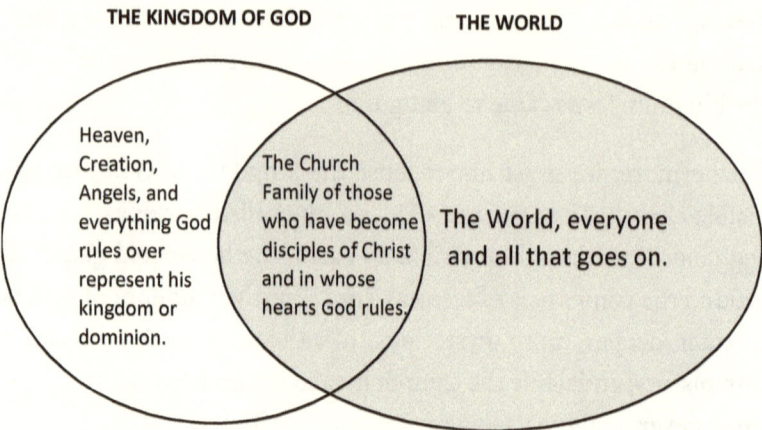

In summing up, we must say this with clarity: the kingdom of God is the reign and dominion of God—his sovereign authority exercised over creation, over history, and, crucially, within the hearts of those who submit to his rule. It is not a place you can pinpoint on a map, nor a political regime you can catalogue. It is the reality of God becoming King—on earth as in heaven—through the life, death, and resurrection of Jesus the Messiah.

The Church, then, is not the kingdom itself but a visible sign of it. It is the called-out people of God—those who have entered into God's household through faith in Christ. They are, as Paul writes, no longer strangers or outsiders but "fellow citizens with God's people and members of his household" (Ephesians 2:19). The Church is that part of the kingdom which has taken root on earth, the advance signpost of what God intends to do for all creation.

To put it plainly: the kingdom is the reign; the Church is the community formed by that reign. The Church lives under God's rule, embodies his values, proclaims his gospel, and awaits the full arrival of his new creation. It is both witness and instrument—a people in whose hearts and lives the kingship of Jesus is already breaking through.

This distinction—between the Church as a visible expression and the kingdom as God's sovereign reign—is critical. It protects us from triumphalism, as though the Church were the full arrival of the kingdom itself. And it guards us against reductionism, as though the kingdom were merely a private, spiritual experience.

Indeed, this understanding gives proper weight to the teaching of salvation in Christ. For it is only through Jesus—the crucified and risen King—that anyone enters the household of God. The Church exists because the kingdom has come near in Jesus, and those who respond in faith become citizens of this new world.

Thus, we affirm: the kingdom of God is far greater than the Church, for it encompasses all of creation under God's reign. And yet the Church, grounded on the truth that Jesus is the Christ, the Son of the living God, is that unique and precious community where the kingdom is already being revealed. It is here, among these called-out ones, that heaven's rule begins to reshape the earth.

The Church

The call to enter the kingdom of God—this new, startling reality that Jesus announces—is not merely a call to adopt a new way of thinking, or to join a religious movement. It is a call to repent: to turn around, to reorient one's life from the path of self and sin toward the reign of the living God, now breaking into the world through the Messiah.

Jesus never presented this as optional. The doorway into the kingdom—into God's renewed people, the Church—is marked first and foremost by repentance, no matter who or where we are when we encounter him. And the Gospel records are filled with encounters that illuminate this kingdom-entry in real time. They are not theoretical illustrations, but vivid portraits of what happens when people come face to face with the King himself.

a) The Paralytic: Faith that Acts (Luke 5:18–24; Matthew 9:2–7)

In one striking episode, friends bring a paralyzed man to Jesus. They do not wait for a convenient path—they dismantle a roof to lower him before the Lord. This is not spectacle; it is faith in motion. And Jesus, seeing not merely the man but the persistent, embodied trust of his friends, says:

> "Take heart, son; your sins are forgiven."

This declaration scandalized the religious minds around him. They accused him—silently—of blasphemy. But Jesus, knowing their thoughts, confronts their inner logic: "Which is easier—to say your sins are forgiven, or to say, 'Get up and walk'?"

And then he offers them the proof:

> "But so that you may know that the Son of Man has authority on earth to forgive sins..." he said to the paralyzed man, "Get up, take your mat, and go home."

The man walks. The crowd marvels. And something of the kingdom breaks through, both in healing and in the declaration of forgiveness. This is not simply a miracle—this is Messianic authority on full display. The kingdom is not about talk; it is about power—grace-filled, restoring, reconciling power. And notice: Jesus meets not only the man's physical affliction but his deeper need—the weight of sin.

Here is faith like Abraham's: not mere belief, but action rooted in trust, regardless of how the outcome may unfold. The friends, the man, and even the crowd are being drawn into the realization that God is now acting in and through Jesus to do what only God can do.

b) The Sinful Woman: Love in Response to Mercy (Luke 7:36–50)

Another scene, no less provocative, unfolds in the home of a Pharisee. Jesus is reclining at the table, and a woman known by reputation—someone the religious elite would consider untouchable—approaches. She does not speak. She weeps. Her tears wash his feet. Her perfume anoints them. Her hair dries them. It is an act of extravagant, almost scandalous devotion.

The Pharisee, observing with judgment, questions Jesus' credibility: "If this man were a prophet, he would know who is touching him..."

But Jesus, once again, reads the heart, and responds not with condemnation but with a parable: two debtors, one forgiven much, the other little. The lesson?

> "Therefore, I tell you, her many sins have been forgiven—as her great love has shown."

And then, the words that echo with divine authority:

> "Your sins are forgiven... Your faith has saved you; go in peace."

The point is clear. It is not religious status that saves, but the posture of the heart before the King. This woman's tears, her gesture of love, are not the price of forgiveness—they are the result of it. Forgiveness is the seed; love is the fruit. Here, once again, Jesus claims the divine prerogative to forgive sin—and does so in a moment of radical, personal, embodied grace. This is the kingdom made visible.

c) The Thief on the Cross: A Kingdom Confession (Luke 23:32–46)

And finally, at the very end of his earthly life, Jesus extends his kingship in perhaps the most unexpected of places: on a Roman cross, between two criminals. One mocks, but the other—stripped of dignity, hanging in agony—utters a confession that has echoed through the centuries:

> *"Jesus, remember me when you come into your kingdom."*

There is no time for long sermons. No ritual. No record of pious deeds. There is only a raw, honest recognition: that this man, broken and bloody beside him, is indeed a king, and that somehow, even in death, his kingdom will endure.

Jesus responds—not with hesitation, not with parable, but with promise:

> *"Truly I tell you, today you will be with me in paradise."*

Here we see the radical nearness of the kingdom of God. It is not a distant realm accessed through years of rule-keeping. It is the gracious invitation of a king who brings the lost home—even from a cross.

And even as darkness falls and the temple curtain is torn, Jesus entrusts himself to the Father: "Into your hands I commit my spirit." (Luke 23:46)

Even in death, he reigns.

So what do we learn from these three moments?

We learn that entry into the kingdom is always marked by a personal, repentant, and faithful encounter with Jesus. It is never earned, but always received in humility. It may happen on a mat, at a dinner table, or on a cross. But always, it requires the same thing: a turning of the heart, and a trusting in the King who alone has the authority to forgive sins and bring us home to God.

This is the good news of the kingdom. And this is how Jesus, even now, continues to call men and women into his household—into the Church, and ultimately, into the life of the age to come.

Why is it that Jesus could forgive the sins of the paralytic, the woman who anointed him, and the thief on the cross? How can this man, walking among the dusty roads of Galilee and Jerusalem, pronounce with such calm authority, "Your sins are forgiven"?

To answer this, we must understand the unfolding story of God's covenant with Israel—a story now reaching its climactic moment in the person of Jesus.

Throughout Israel's history, the forgiveness of sins was inseparably tied to the temple, to priesthood, and to sacrificial blood. Sins were atoned for through the shedding of animal blood, administered through the proper rituals, as a temporary provision under the Law. Yet, as the prophets made clear, this system pointed beyond itself to a future reality when God would at last deal decisively with sin—not merely through ritual, but through a final act of redemption.

Enter Jesus.

Jesus does not abolish the Law or the sacrificial system; he fulfills them. As he walks the earth, healing the sick and welcoming sinners, he does so as Israel's Messiah and the embodiment of Yahweh himself. He is the true temple in person, the true high priest, and ultimately, the true sacrificial offering. Thus, when he forgives sins during his earthly ministry, he does so by divine authority. His pronouncement is not blasphemy—it is kingdom-breaking-in reality.

> *"But so that you may know that the Son of Man has authority on earth to forgive sins..." (Matthew 9:6)*

Jesus knew where his mission was heading. His authority to forgive sins did not exist in isolation—it pointed forward to the cross. There, in his crucifixion, the entire sacrificial narrative of Israel would find its fulfillment. His death was not merely tragic; it was atoning. His blood, as the writer to the Hebrews declares, inaugurated the New Covenant (Hebrews 9:12–14).

And with the resurrection came vindication: God had acted in history to conquer sin and death, to establish a new creation, and to announce that Jesus—crucified and risen—is Lord of all.

So, while Jesus forgave sins during his earthly life as the authorized agent of God's reign, the power behind that forgiveness was ultimately grounded in what he would accomplish on the cross. His shed blood became the basis, once and for all, by which forgiveness is extended to all who turn to him.

> *"This is my blood of the covenant, which is poured out for many for the forgiveness of sins." (Matthew 26:28)*

After the resurrection, Jesus commissions his followers not only to proclaim the kingdom but to offer this very forgiveness—through his name, in the power of the Spirit, to all nations (Luke 24:47; Acts 2:38). The new covenant had dawned, and with it, a new way of entering into the household of God. And as we shall soon explore, no one illustrates this shift more profoundly than Saul of Tarsus—persecutor turned apostle, whose encounter with the risen Jesus on the road to Damascus would both exemplify and proclaim the new reality of salvation through the crucified and risen King.

WHAT MUST I DO TO BE SAVED?

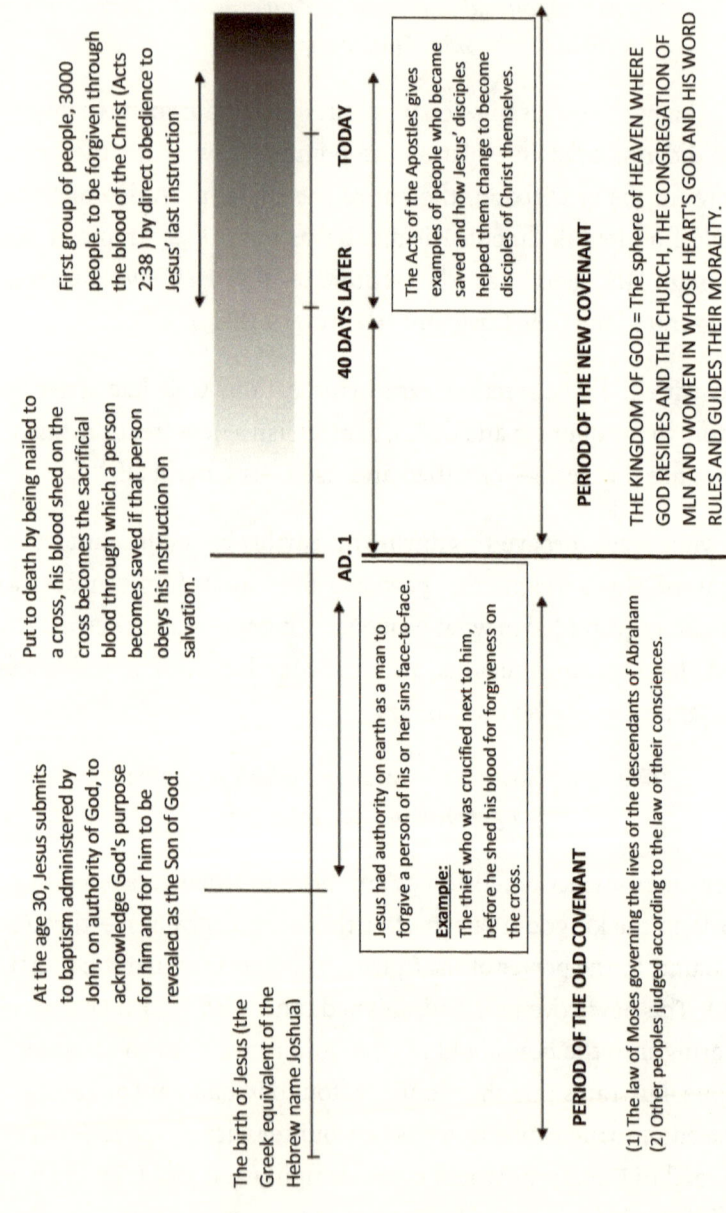

The birth of Jesus (the Greek equivalent of the Hebrew name Joshua)

At the age 30, Jesus submits to baptism administered by John, on authority of God, to acknowledge God's purpose for him and for him to be revealed as the Son of God.

Put to death by being nailed to a cross, his blood shed on the cross becomes the sacrificial blood through which a person becomes saved if that person obeys his instruction on salvation.

First group of people, 3000 people. to be forgiven through the blood of the Christ (Acts 2:38) by direct obedience to Jesus' last instruction

AD. 1   40 DAYS LATER   TODAY

Jesus had authority on earth as a man to forgive a person of his or her sins face-to-face.

Example:
The thief who was crucified next to him, before he shed his blood for forgiveness on the cross.

The Acts of the Apostles gives examples of people who became saved and how Jesus' disciples helped them change to become disciples of Christ themselves.

PERIOD OF THE OLD COVENANT

(1) The law of Moses governing the lives of the descendants of Abraham
(2) Other peoples judged according to the law of their consciences.

PERIOD OF THE NEW COVENANT

THE KINGDOM OF GOD = The sphere of HEAVEN WHERE GOD RESIDES AND THE CHURCH, THE CONGREGATION OF MEN AND WOMEN IN WHOSE HEART'S GOD AND HIS WORD RULES AND GUIDES THEIR MORALITY.

95

What Must I Do to Live Forever in Heaven?

It is a question that echoes through the ages, asked not only by religious scholars in Jesus' day but by thoughtful seekers in every generation: "What must I do to inherit eternal life?" (Luke 10:25). The question came from an expert in the Law—a man steeped in the Scriptures, a teacher of Israel. And yet his question, though clothed in testing, reveals something deeply human: a longing to know what it means to truly live, both now and into the age to come.

Jesus, as so often, does not answer the question directly, but draws the man back to the source. "What is written in the Law? How do you read it?" (Luke 10:26). The man replies with what every devout Jew would know by heart, drawn from the Shema and the Holiness Code: "Love the Lord your God with all your heart, soul, strength, and mind; and love your neighbor as yourself." (Luke 10:27).

Jesus affirms the answer. "You have answered correctly," he says. "Do this, and you will live." (Luke 10:28)

Here we glimpse the heart of Jesus' teaching—not a rejection of Israel's tradition, but its true fulfillment. The way into life, eternal life, is not found in abstract belief or ritual performance. It begins with covenant love—a total devotion to God, and a life poured out in generosity and mercy toward one's fellow human beings. This, Jesus says, is the road that leads to life.

But this is not merely a theological statement. It is a window into the kingdom. Jesus' teaching, and the stories he tells, invite us to understand that eternal life is not simply a post-mortem destination called "heaven," but a quality of life, a reality of the new creation, breaking into the present age. And this life is shaped by fidelity to God's purposes and by the self-giving love that marks those who belong to his kingdom.

Let us look at how Jesus expands and deepens this reality through a series of encounters and teachings—moments where the question of salvation is not posed abstractly, but lived out in the real stories of ordinary people.

On one occasion, someone asks him, "Lord, are only a few people going to be saved?" (Luke 13:23). Jesus responds with a challenge that turns mere curiosity into personal urgency:

> "Make every effort to enter through the narrow door, because many, I tell you, will try to enter and will not be able to..." (Luke 13:24)

Jesus is not interested in theoretical speculation. He is calling for decisive action. The door to the kingdom is narrow—not because God is stingy, but because the call is serious. It is not about association with Jesus—"We ate and drank with you"—but about allegiance to him. Not familiarity, but fidelity.

And then, in a reversal typical of the kingdom, Jesus says that "people will come from east and west and north and south, and will take their places at the feast in the kingdom of God." (Luke 13:29). Those who assumed they were on the inside may find themselves outside, while others, seemingly far from the covenant, are welcomed in.

This is not simply a warning—it is an invitation. Jesus is redrawing the boundaries of God's people around himself. The kingdom is arriving, and the door is open, but it must be entered through repentance, humility, and faithfulness.

And so we return to the original question: "What must I do to inherit eternal life?" Jesus answers: Love God. Love your neighbor. Enter by the narrow door. Live in alignment with the reign of God. This is not about escaping the world, but about entering into God's new world, a world being born in and through Jesus himself.

This is the way of salvation. This is the life of the age to come. And it begins now.

He Who Does the Will of God

In one of Jesus' most searching teachings, found near the end of the Sermon on the Mount, he confronts a tendency that spans every generation: the temptation to substitute religious performance for covenant obedience.

> "Not everyone who says to me, 'Lord, Lord,' will enter the kingdom of heaven, but only he who does the will of my Father who is in heaven." (Matthew 7:21)

This is no small statement. Here is Jesus, not simply offering moral instruction, but placing himself in the position of final judgment, the one before whom all humanity must give account. And what does he say will matter? Not spiritual achievement. Not even supernatural acts done in his name. What matters is doing the will of the Father.

Many, Jesus says, will claim to have known him. They will point to their ministries, their miracles, their teachings. And yet he will reply, "I never knew you. Away from me, you evildoers!" (Matthew 7:23)

This is not a rejection of outward signs of faith. Rather, it is a warning against a spirituality disconnected from obedience. The kingdom of God is not interested in mere words or impressive acts; it is about becoming the kind of person through whom God's will is done on earth as it is in heaven.

Jesus is not saying that good works save. He is saying that true allegiance to him is always evidenced by obedience to the will of God—the kind of obedience that flows from a heart transformed by grace. This is the life built on rock, not sand. And this is the kind of life that endures.

Morally Good is Not Enough

Elsewhere, we meet a man who might, by all accounts, be considered exemplary. A young ruler, both wealthy and devout, comes to Jesus with the ultimate question:

> *"Teacher, what good thing must I do to get eternal life?"* (Matthew 19:16)

Jesus begins by directing him to the commandments—the heart of Israel's moral and social life. The man replies, almost with relief: "All these I have kept since I was a boy." But Jesus sees deeper. He looks beyond moral decency and asks for something more radical:

> *"If you want to be perfect, go, sell your possessions and give to the poor, and you will have treasure in heaven. Then come, follow me."* (Matthew 19:21)

And with that, the man walks away, sorrowful.

The tragedy of this encounter is not that the man was sinful, but that he was unwilling to let go. He had obeyed the rules, yes. But Jesus was calling him not simply to moral uprightness, but to covenant loyalty—to trust, to surrender, to a new way of life rooted in the values of the kingdom.

Here, as elsewhere, Jesus is not offering a generic moral code. He is proclaiming the arrival of God's reign, and inviting people to reorder their lives around that reality. The call to "follow me" is not a supplement to righteousness—it is the fulfillment of it.

This man had everything, and yet lacked the one thing necessary: a heart willing to release its grip on worldly security in order to take hold of eternal life—the life of the age to come, now breaking into the present through Jesus.

In both these passages, we see a profound truth: that eternal life is not a prize for good behavior or public religiosity. It is the life of God's new world, offered to those who align themselves with his will, who recognize Jesus not simply as "Lord" in name but as the very embodiment of God's kingdom in action. To inherit that life is to live it now—in humility, in trust, and in obedience.

Must Give Up Everything...

Jesus never recruited followers under false pretenses. He did not appeal to the crowds with promises of comfort or prosperity. Quite the opposite. As the crowds grew, so did the gravity of his call:

> *"If anyone comes to me and does not hate his father and mother, his wife and children, his brothers and sisters—yes, even his own life—he cannot be my disciple. And anyone who does not carry his cross and follow me cannot be my disciple."* (Luke 14:26–27)

These words shock the modern ear, but they were no less startling in the first century. Jesus is using prophetic hyperbole—common in Jewish teaching—not to promote animosity, but to reorder allegiance. The point is clear: if loyalty to family, comfort, or even one's own life stands in the way of following him, then the kingdom has not yet taken root in the heart.

This is not about emotional detachment; it is about the radical realignment of our entire being around the lordship of Christ. The cross is not merely an instrument of death; it becomes the symbol of discipleship—the path of self-denial, love, and faithfulness in the face of suffering. Jesus' call is not simply to believe, but to follow, even when it costs everything.

> *"Anyone who loves father or mother more than me is not worthy of me... and anyone who does not take up his cross and follow me is not worthy of me."* (Matthew 10:37–38)

This is not an additional burden placed upon us; it is the shape of the kingdom life itself—a life that is cruciform, because it mirrors the very pattern of Christ's own love.

Being About the Lord's Business...

Jesus not only called people into a new way of life, but also pointed ahead to a future day of reckoning—a day when God's justice would be fully unveiled, and the hidden faithfulness of his people made known:

> *"When the Son of Man comes in his glory... he will separate the people one from another as a shepherd separates the sheep from the goats." (Matthew 25:31–32)*

This is a scene not of arbitrary judgment, but of profound moral accountability. The King does not ask about creeds or titles. He speaks instead of food and drink, of hospitality and compassion, of care for the sick and imprisoned. The great surprise is not just who is welcomed in, but why: they served Christ by serving "the least of these."

> *"Whatever you did for one of the least of these brothers of mine, you did for me." (Matthew 25:40)*

This is not salvation by works, but a clear declaration that those who belong to the kingdom live out its values—not to earn grace, but because they have been transformed by it. This is what it means to be about the Father's business: not just professing Jesus as Lord, but embodying his mercy in the world.

And those who fail to do so—those who neglect the hungry, the stranger, the suffering—reveal not a lapse in ethics but a failure of allegiance. For to ignore the vulnerable is, in the eyes of the King, to ignore him.

The Promised Spirit—For Those Who Obey

The call to follow Jesus, to live under his lordship, to serve others as though serving him—it might seem impossible. And it would be, were it not for the promised gift:

> *"If you love me, you will obey what I command. And I will ask the Father, and he will give you another Counselor to be with you forever—the Spirit of truth."* (John 14:15–17)

Here Jesus assures his disciples that he will not leave them orphaned. The life of obedience he calls them to is not one they live in their own strength. Rather, the Holy Spirit—the very life and breath of God—will dwell with them, and indeed, within them.

But there is a condition: "Whoever has my commands and obeys them, he is the one who loves me." (John 14:21)

Love and obedience are not rivals in the kingdom of God; they are inseparable. The Spirit is given not as a spiritual perk, but as the presence of God empowering faithfulness. And with the Spirit comes the mutual indwelling Jesus promises: "I am in my Father, and you are in me, and I am in you." (John 14:20)

This is the astonishing reality of new covenant life: the life of God taking up residence in human hearts, forming a new kind of people—obedient, Spirit-filled, and marked by love. And to such people, Jesus says, "My Father will love him, and we will come to him and make our home with him." (John 14:23)

The kingdom has drawn near. The King is calling. The Spirit is ready. The question that remains is the one we must each answer: Will we follow?

His Final Instruction

The risen Jesus stood before his disciples, bearing the marks of crucifixion and the glory of resurrection. The long story of Israel had reached its decisive turning point. The powers of sin and death had been broken. A new creation had begun. And with divine authority, Jesus now issues the commission that would launch a global movement:

> *"All authority in heaven and on earth has been given to me. Therefore, go and make disciples of all nations, baptizing them in the name of the Father and of the Son and of the Holy Spirit, and teaching them to obey everything I have commanded you. And surely, I am with you always, to the very end of the age." (Matthew 28:18–20)*

This is no mere epilogue. It is the climax of the Gospel story and the beginning of a new chapter in God's redemptive plan. The One who now bears all authority sends his followers not simply to make converts or gather adherents, but to make disciples—people formed in his likeness, brought into the life of the Triune God, and taught to walk in obedience.

This final instruction reveals the desire of God's heart: that all people—every tribe, every tongue—might come to know his Son, receive his Spirit, and be restored into his image. It is the will of God that each person be baptized, that each be taught, and that each walk in obedience to Jesus' way—the way of the cross, the way of love, the way of new creation.

But note how Jesus frames it: the command to baptize is not isolated from teaching, nor detached from faith. Baptism, in this commission, is not an empty rite, nor a mere symbol. It is an embodied act of allegiance, the visible sign of entry into the kingdom of God, and it is always to be joined with teaching that forms lives shaped by Jesus' commands.

As the early church would soon proclaim:

> "There is salvation in no one else, for there is no other name under heaven given among men by which we must be saved." (Acts 4:12)

And again, echoing Jesus' own words:

> "He who believes and is baptized will be saved, but he who does not believe will be condemned." (Mark 16:16)

This is not a mechanical formula. It is the unveiling of how salvation takes root. Faith and baptism belong together, not as competing signs, but as mutually reinforcing acts of obedience. Baptism is not something one performs for oneself—it is a moment of surrender, of being named and claimed by the God whose love raised Jesus from the dead.

And so it is fitting that, in the story of Saul of Tarsus, we find precisely this pattern. Though Jesus himself met Saul on the road, it was through the obedient faith of another—Ananias—that the message was preached and baptism offered. Saul did not baptize himself. He submitted to the gospel, and in doing so, was baptized—dying to the old creation and rising into the new (Acts 22:16).

This is the rhythm of the Church's mission: proclaim the good news, call people to trust, baptize them into the life of the Triune God, and teach them to live in obedience to Jesus, the world's true Lord.

And Jesus is with us—not merely in memory or principle, but in presence and power, until the day the whole earth is filled with the knowledge of the Lord as the waters cover the sea.

5

What Peter & the Apostles taught

From what we've observed so far, it becomes ever clearer that the pathway to answering the deeply personal and eternally significant question, "What must I do to be saved?" begins not with allegiance to human traditions or extra-biblical regulations, but with a posture of humility and obedience to the God-breathed Scriptures themselves. This is where the story always begins—not in the speculative abstractions of religion, but in the concrete call of God breaking into history.

Let us consider the scene at the Jordan River. Before Jesus so much as uttered a parable or performed a miracle, there stood John the Baptist, thundering a call to repentance. His was no vague spiritual sentiment, but a specific summons to turn from real, identifiable sins and step into the waters of baptism—a symbolic but powerfully real act of submission and new beginning. And yet, remarkably, some of the most religiously learned of the day refused. They stood aloof, making the same tragic misstep as Naaman the Syrian, who nearly let pride and presumption bar the way to healing. Only, unlike Naaman, they had no Elisha figure urging them to wisdom.

Then Jesus arrived—not to stand aloof, but to plunge into those very waters. He identified himself fully with this movement of repentance and renewal. The Gospel writers tell us what happened next: "the heavens opened, and the Spirit of God descended upon him and testified that he was the Son of God." At that moment, every excuse melted away for those who presumed to stand above John's message. The divine endorsement was not merely a dramatic sign—it was an eschatological declaration. The kingdom was at hand, and its King had arrived.

Yet even then, not all responded. Some heard John and turned away. Others encountered Jesus himself—and still refused his call to repent. The dilemma remains the same in our day. It is not that we are uniquely wicked, but that we are being confronted with something radical and deeply unfamiliar: a message not born from human tradition, but from the very heart of God. Whether we were raised in alternative religious traditions or formed by personal beliefs that do not align with the revelation of the Son of God, we are now faced with a decision that only we can make.

As Jesus himself explained, the issue is not one of intellect but of the heart's disposition. The problem is not a lack of data, but a resistance to transformation. This is why, when asked why he spoke in parables, Jesus responded:

> *"This is the reason I speak to them in figures, because they see and yet cannot perceive; and they hear and yet do not listen, nor do they understand. And in them is fulfilled the prophecy of Isaiah who said, 'Hearing you will hear, but you will not understand; and seeing you will see, but you will not know. For the heart of this people has become hardened, and they hear with difficulty, and their eyes are dull; so that they cannot see with their eyes, and hear with their ears, and understand with their hearts; let them return, and I will heal them.'"*
>
> —Matthew 13:13–15

Indeed, at the heart of much modern misunderstanding is a form of contextomy—a tearing of verses out of their narrative home and theological soil. This is, fundamentally, a failure of humility. If we cannot submit ourselves to the Scriptures' call—if we cannot begin with the fundamental act of repentance—then the question of salvation becomes, for us, not a theological pursuit but a veiled resistance to the truth. Salvation is not gained by mastering a system but by the heart's awakening to God's gracious initiative.

So then, let us look forward. After Jesus' resurrection, he did not leave this calling as a vague ideal. He entrusted it to real people—men and women who had walked with him, eaten with him, wept and rejoiced with him. To these first followers, he gave final instructions concerning the shape of salvation and the means by which his message would carry forward into the world. These were not theoretical disciples, but flesh-and-blood witnesses who bore the gospel not only in word but in life.

Let us, then, attend closely to their lives and testimonies. For in their footsteps, we find the first echoes of the church's mission—and the ongoing call to you and to me: "Come, follow me."

Those called by Jesus to be apostles.

FIRST GROUP	
Peter: given name Simon, changed to Cephas (Aramaic), or Peter (Greek): native of Bethsaida: son of John, brother of Andrew; fisherman, home in Capernaum: present at transfiguration and Gethsemane; denied Christ; first apostle to (1) preach the gospel. (2) perform a miracle, (3) speak before the Sanhedrin, (4) preach to Gentiles, (5) raise the dead; traditionally martyred at Rome in AD. 67	Too extensive to list but note Gal 2:7-9; 1. 2 Peter.
Andrew: introduced brother Peter to Jesus: son of John: native of Bethsaida: fisherman; traditionally martyred in Greece; brought word to Jesus of Greeks who wanted to see him.	Matt. 4:18; 10:2; Mark 1:16, 29; 3:18; 13:3; Luke 6:14: John 1:40, 44; 6:8; 12:22: Acts 1:13
James: brother of John: son of Zebedee and Salome; fisherman. with father and brother partners with Peter: present ot transfiguration and in Gethsemane: called by Jesus a "Son of Thunder": martyred by Herod Agrippa I (c. A.D. 44)	Matt, 4:21: 10:2; 17:1; Mark 1:19, 29: 3:17; 5:37; 9:2: 10:35, 41: 13:3; 14:33; Luke 5:10; 6:14; 8:51: 9:28, 54; Aas 1:13; 12:2
John: brother of James; son of Zebedee and Salome: fisherman, partner with Peter: present at transfiguration and in Gethsemane: called by Jesus "Son of Thunder'; "the disciple whom Jesus loved": companion of Peter: cared for Mary, the Lord's mother; leader in Jerusalem church; later moved to Ephesus; exited to isle of Patmos; traditionally not martyred	Matt. 4:21; 10:2; 17:1; Mark 1:19, 29: 3:17; 5:37; 9:2, 38; 10:35, 41: 13:3: 14:33; Luke 5:10; 6:14; 8:51; 9:28, 49, 54; 22:8; Acts 1:13: 3:1, 3, 4, 11: 4:13, 19; 8:14; 12:2; Gal. 2:9; Rev. 1:1, 4, 9; 22:8. C& 1, 2. 3 John. Gospel of John.

WHAT MUST I DO TO BE SAVED?

SECOND GROUP	
Philip: native of Bethsaida: told Nathanael of Jesus; brought word to Jesus of Greeks who wanted to see Him; traditions unclear	Matt. 10:3: Mark 3:18; Luke 6:14: John 1:43-46, 48; 6:5, 7; 12:21-22; 14:8-9; Acts 1:13
Bartholomew: probably Nathanael of John's Gospel; from Cana; name Bartholomew Aramaic for "Son of Tolmai"; Jesus saw him under the fig tree: traditionally martyred in Armenia	Matt. 10:3; Mark 3:18: Luke 6:14; John 1:45-49; 21:2; Acts 1:13
Thomas (called Didymus): probably from Galilee; asked Jesus how to know the way: doubted Jesus' resurrection: traditionally preached in India	Matt. 10:3: Mark 3:18; Luke 6:15; John 13:16; 14:5; 20:24, 26-28; 21:2: Acts 1:13
Matthew: tax collector: son of Alphsecus: also known as Levi, held a great feast for Jesus in his house; tradition unclear.	Matt. 9:9; 10:3; Mark 2:14; 3:18; Luke 5:27. 29: 6:15; Acts 1:13
THIRD GROUP	
James: son of Alphaeus and Mary; known as the "small" or "the Younger'; brother of Joseph: tradition unclear due to confusion with other Jameses	Mott. 10:3; 27.56; Mark 3:18; 15:40; 16:1; Luke 6:15; 24:10; Acts 1:13
Judas (not Iscariot): son of James; also ce led Thaddseus; perhaps a Zealot: traditionally preached in Armenia and martyred in Persia with Simon the Zealot	Matt. 10:3; Mark 3:18: Luke 6:16; John 14:22; Acts 1:13
Simon the Zealot: traditionally martyred in Persia with Jude	Mott. 10:4; Mark 3:18; Luke 6:15; Acts 1:13
Judas Iscariot: possibly from Judea; betrayer of Christ: ca led by Jesus "devil" and "son of perdition"; treasurer for the apostolic band: committed suicide	Matt. 10:4: 26:14, 25, 47; 27:3, 5; Maric 3:19; 14:10, 43; Luke 6:16; 22:3. 47, 48; John 6:71; 12:4; 13:2, 26, 29; 18:2, 3, 5; Acts 1:16, 18, 25

"He appointed twelve—designating them apostles—that they might be with him and that he might send them out to preach and to have authority to drive out demons."

—*Mark 3:13–19*

Here, then, is the beginning of the new Israel. Just as the twelve tribes once formed the foundation of God's covenant people, so now Jesus reconstitutes the people of God around himself. This is not mere symbolism—it is a living, breathing, revolutionary act. These twelve are not merely followers; they are those through whom the Messiah will launch his new creation project. Each of them, with all their quirks, flaws, and strengths, becomes part of the architecture of God's redemptive plan.

1. Simon Peter, the man of rock – Impetuous, bold, often stumbling yet chosen to be the steady foundation. Not because of who he was in himself, but because of what grace would make of him.
2. Andrew, Peter's brother – The quiet evangelist. The one who brings others to Jesus, even when he stands in the shadow of his more prominent brother.
3. James, son of Zebedee, and
4. John, his brother – The sons of thunder. Fiery, passionate, quick to call down judgment. Yet John, by the end, becomes the apostle of love. This is the transforming power of walking with the Christ.
5. Philip, the earnest inquirer – Ever asking, ever seeking. "Show us the Father," he once said—and in so doing voiced the yearning of Israel's long hope.
6. Bartholomew, also known as Nathaniel, the guileless Israelite – In him, Jesus saw a heart without deceit. A man whose quiet integrity became the soil in which the truth could take root.
7. Thomas, the melancholic – Often remembered for his doubt, but he gave one of the most profound confessions:

"My Lord and my God." His skepticism led not to cynicism, but to deeper faith.
8. Matthew, the publican – A tax collector, collaborator with the empire. Yet Jesus calls him, sits at his table, and transforms him into a chronicler of the kingdom.
9. James, son of Alphaeus – A quiet figure in the gospel narratives, yet no less part of the foundation. God's kingdom often advances through those the world overlooks.
10. Thaddaeus, also known as Lebbaeus or Judas, son of James – The disciple of many names. Sometimes hidden, sometimes mysterious. A reminder that the gospel is carried forward by both the known and the obscure.
11. Simon, the Zealot – Once aligned with violent revolution, now a follower of the Prince of Peace. A living testimony to how Jesus redefines kingdom and power.
12. Judas Iscariot, the man of Kerioth – The one who betrayed him. Even he was called, even he was sent out. A tragic figure, and a warning: proximity to Jesus is not the same as loyalty to him.

These twelve, in all their diversity, are the first-fruits of the new humanity Jesus is forming. Not spiritual superheroes, but ordinary men reoriented by grace. Their story is not simply history—it is a pattern, a template, a calling that echoes still.

These twelve men—ordinary yet extraordinary—were appointed by Jesus not simply as assistants in a religious campaign, but as the first witnesses of the risen Lord (Luke 24:48; Acts 1:8). They are, in the vision of the New Jerusalem, inscribed on the twelve foundational stones (Revelation 21:14). This is no mere symbolism;

it is the architecture of new creation. These were the ones who heard Jesus' teaching with their own ears, saw his miracles with their own eyes, and received his final charge to bring the good news of the kingdom to the ends of the earth. Jesus called them out from the crowds—and they responded.

To understand what this call looks like, what kind of transformation it demands, we do well to return to one of Jesus' most famous parables—the story of the Lost Son (Luke 15). Here, Jesus reveals not only the nature of repentance, but the very heart of the Father. The son, weary and wasted, returns not to judgment, but to the embrace of a father who has been waiting all along. This is not simply a tale of moral failure and recovery; it is the story of Israel, the story of humanity, the story of you and me.

And remarkably, this story finds distant echoes in the traditions of other nations. From the Lotus Sutra, a sacred text within the Vedic heritage, we hear a story told centuries before Jesus' birth—of a son who abandons his father, wanders for decades in poverty and confusion, only to be slowly and patiently drawn back by the father's compassion. At first, the son cannot comprehend the father's love. He sees only a powerful figure to be feared. He is content to clean the filth from the master's house, not realizing he is working in his own inheritance.

> *It is like the case of a boy who, when still young, without understanding, abandoned his father and ran away, going far off to another land, drifting from one country to another for over fifty years. His father, distressed in thought, searched for him in every direction till, worn out with searching, he halted in a certain city. There he built a*

dwelling where he could indulge the five desires. His house was large and costly, with quantities of gold, silver, seashell, agate, pearls, lapis lazuli, elephants, horses, oxen, goats, palanquins, and carriages, fields for farming, menservants, grooms, and other people in great number.

He engaged in profitable ventures at home and in all the lands around and had merchants and traveling vendors stationed everywhere. Thousands, ten thousand, millions surrounded him and paid reverence; he enjoyed the constant favor and consideration of the ruler. The officials and powerful clans all joined in paying him honor, and those who for one reason or another flocked about him were many. Such was his vast wealth, the great power and influence he possessed.

But as he grew old and decrepit, he recalled his son with greater distress than ever, day and night thinking of nothing else:

"Now the time of my death draws near. Over fifty years have passed since that foolish boy abandoned me. My storehouses full of goods— what will become of them?" At this time, the impoverished son was searching for food and clothing, going from village to village, from country to country, sometimes finding something, other times finding nothing, starving and emaciated, his body broken out in sores and ringworm. As he moved from place to place, he arrived in time at the city where his father lived, shifting from one job to another until he came to his father's house.

WHAT MUST I DO TO BE SAVED?

At that time, the rich man had spread a large, jeweled canopy inside his gate and was seated on a lion throne, surrounded by his dependents and various attendants and guards. Some were counting out gold, silver, and precious objects, or recording in ledgers the outlay and income of wealth. The impoverished son, observing how eminent and distinguished his father was, supposed he must be the king of a country or the equal of a king. Alarmed and full of wonder, he asked himself why he had come here. Secretly he thought to himself, If I linger here for long, I will perhaps be seized and pressed into service! Once this thought had occurred to him, he raced from the spot, and inquiring where there was a poor village, went there in hopes of gaining employment. The rich man at the time, seated on his lion throne, saw his son in the distance and silently recognized who he was. Immediately he instructed a messenger to hurry after him and bring him back. The impoverished son, crying out in terror, sank to the ground in distress.

"This man has seized me and is surely going to put me to death! To think that my search for food and clothing should bring me to this!" The rich man knew that his son was ignorant and self-abasing. "He will never believe my words; will never believe I am his father."

So he employed an expedient means, sending some other men to the son, a one-eyed man, another puny and uncouth, completely lacking in imposing appearance, saying, "Speak to him and tell him I will employ him to remove excrement and filth, and will pay him twice the regular wage."

When the impoverished son heard this, he was delighted and came with the messengers and worked to clear away excrement and filth and clean the rooms of the house. From the window the rich man would constantly observe his son, thinking how his son was ignorant and self-abasing and delighted in such menial labor. At such times, the rich man would put on dirty ragged clothing, take in hand a utensil for removing excrement and go to where his son was, using this expedient means to approach him, encouraging him to work diligently.

"I have increased your wages and given you more oil to rub on your feet. I will see that you have plenty to eat and drink, mats and bedding that are thick and warm." At times he would speak severely: "You must work hard!" Or again he would say in a gentle voice, "You are like a son to me."

The rich man, being wise, gradually permitted his son to come and go in the house. And after twenty years had passed, he put him in charge of household affairs, showing him his gold, silver, pearls, crystal, and the other things that were handed out or gathered in, so that he would understand all about them, though the son continued to live outside the gate, sleeping in a hut of grass, for he looked upon himself as poor, thinking, "None of these things are mine." The father knew that his son's outlook was gradually becoming broader and more magnanimous, and, wishing to hand over his wealth and goods, he called *together his relatives, the king of the country and the high ministers, the noblemen and householders.*

In the presence of this great assembly he declared, "This is my son who abandoned me and wandered abroad for a period of fifty years. Since I found him again, twenty years have gone by. Long ago, in such-and-such a city, when I lost my son, I traveled all around searching for him until eventually I came here. All that I possess, my house and people, I hand over entirely to him so he may do with them as he wishes." The son thought how in the past he had been poor, humble and self-abasing in outlook, but now he had received from his father this huge bequest of rare treasures, along with the father's house and all his wealth and goods.

He was filled with great joy, having gained what he never had before.

LOTUS SUTRA 4

This parable, though separated from the gospel by time, language, and theology, shows something profound about the human condition. It bears witness to a universal ache—the longing for home, the lostness of humanity, and the patient mercy of one who does not forget his children.

But it is in Jesus, and only in Jesus, that this archetypal yearning finds its fulfillment. In his own telling of the Lost Son, Jesus reframes the entire drama of Israel and the world: the younger son, representing the outcasts and "sinners," returns home and is embraced; the elder son, like the Pharisees, remains outside, offended at grace. The Father's house is open to both, yet neither understands it fully. And yet, here is the difference—Jesus is not just telling a story. He is living it.

In Christ, the Father is not distant or hidden behind layers of parable and palace gates. No, the Word became flesh and dwelt among us. The one seated on heaven's throne came not with jewels and elephants, but with sandals and scars. He stooped not in disguise, but in divine humility, washing feet, touching lepers, embracing the broken.

And unlike the Vedic tale, in which the father waits for recognition across years and strategies, the gospel announces that God himself came running—arms wide, robes flying, interrupting our shame with a kiss and a ring and a feast. This is the scandal of grace, the joy of the gospel, and the mission of the twelve: to proclaim that the Father has not forgotten his children, that the lost are being found, and that the whole cosmos is being renewed through the death and resurrection of the Son.

So when we hear stories, ancient or modern, that speak of estrangement and return, we recognize in them the longings planted in every human heart. But in Jesus Christ, those longings are no longer whispers in the dark. They have found their answer. The lost son is welcomed. The door to the house stands open. The feast has begun.

Jesus concludes his telling of the Lost Son not with sentimental warmth, but with a stark and joyful clarity: "It was right to celebrate and be glad, for this brother of yours was dead, and is alive again; he was lost, and is found." The return home, the embrace, the feast—this is not merely a touching ending. It is a summons to see that repentance is the gateway into resurrection life, and that joy in heaven is not theoretical—it breaks out in song when the lost are found.

But let us not miss what Jesus is truly saying here. This story is not an abstract parable. It is the very heart of the gospel: a call to return, to repent, to obey. Because for Jesus, the invitation into the Father's house is not issued apart from the call to obedience. The one who tells this story is the same one who would say—without hesitation and without compromise:

> "Not everyone who says to me, 'My Lord, my Lord,' will enter into the kingdom of heaven, but only the one who does the will of my Father in heaven.
>
> Many will say to me on that day, 'Lord, Lord, did we not prophesy in your name, cast out demons, and perform many wonders?'
>
> Then I will declare to them, 'I never knew you. Depart from me, you workers of lawlessness.'"
>
> —Matthew 7:21–23

These are not peripheral words. They form the conclusion of the Sermon on the Mount—the very heart of Jesus' kingdom manifesto. Jesus is not simply offering advice; he is announcing a new reality, the arrival of God's reign on earth as in heaven. And within that new reality, the decisive question is not merely, "Did you hear what Jesus said?" but, "Did you live by it?"

> "Everyone, then, who hears these words of mine and puts them into practice," Jesus continues, "is like a wise man who built his house on the rock." (v. 24)

The storm, the flood, the winds—they come to both houses. The difference is not in the weather, but in the foundation. The rock is not intellectual agreement or religious enthusiasm—it is obedience to the way of Jesus, to the will of the Father, revealed and embodied in the Son.

And what of those who hear but do not do?

"They are like the foolish man who built his house on sand." (v. 26)

The language is clear—and sobering. The fall is not minor, but "great." This is no petty collapse; it is a catastrophic reckoning for a life built on performance rather than trust, on appearances rather than obedience.

So then, the question, "What must I do to be saved?", is not answered by clever interpretation or religious assumption. It is answered in the daily doing of what Jesus teaches. There is no salvation apart from him—not merely believing in his name, but entrusting one's life to his voice, his commands, his path.

In the end, it is not merely about calling him "Lord," but allowing him to actually be Lord—of our time, our priorities, our desires, our very selves.

For the kingdom of God is not a theoretical hope—it is a present reality that demands a response. You can obey, and find your life built on the rock, unshaken in the storm. Or you can reinterpret, delay, or resist—and discover too late that your foundation could not stand.

The choice is yours. But Jesus has already spoken. The Father is already running. The feast is already being prepared.

Jesus' final instruction to the 11 apostles

The Good News according to Matthew

ON the evening of the sabbath, when the first day of the week began, there came Mary of Magdala and the other Mary, to see the tomb.

2 And behold, a great earthquake took place; for the angel of the Lord came down from heaven, and went up and rolled away the stone from the door, and sat on it. 3 His appearance was like lightning, and his garments were white as snow. 4 And for fear of him the guards who were watching trembled and became as if they were dead. 5 But the angel answered and said to the women, You need not be afraid; for I know that you are seeking Jesus who

The Good News according to Mark

WHEN the sabbath had passed, Mary of Magdala, and Mary the mother of James, and Salome, bought spices, that they might come and anoint him. 2 Early in the morning, on the first day of the week, they came to the tomb as the sun was just rising. 3 And they said among themselves, Who will roll away the stone from the door of the tomb for us? 4 And they looked and saw that the stone was rolled away, for it was very large. 5 And they entered the tomb, and saw a young man, sitting on the right, covered with a white robe; and they were astonished. 6 But he said to them, Do not be afraid. You seek Jesus the Nazarene, was crucified. 6 He is not here, for he has risen, just as he had said. Come, see the place where our Lord was laid. 7 And go quickly, and tell his disciples that he has risen from the dead; and behold, he will go before you to Galilee; there you will see him; lo, I have told you. 8 And they went away hurriedly from the tomb with fear and with great joy, running to tell his disciples. 9 And behold, Jesus met them and said to them, Peace be to you. And they came up and laid hold of his feet, and worshipped him.

10 Then Jesus said to them, Do not be afraid; but go and tell my brethren to go to Galilee, and there they shall see me. 11 While they were going, some of the guards came into the city, and told the high priests everything that had happened. 12 So they gathered with the elders and

who was crucified; he has risen; he is not here; behold the place where he was laid. 7 But go away and tell his disciples, and Peter, that he will be before you in Galilee; there you will see him, just as he has told you. 8 And when they heard it, they fled and went out of the tomb, for they were seized with amazement and trembling; and they said nothing to any man, for they were frightened. 9 1] Now he rose early on the first day of the week, and appeared first to Mary of Magdala, from whom he had cast seven demons.

10 And she went and brought glad tidings to those who were with him, who now were mourning and weeping. 11 And when they heard them saying that he was alive, and had appeared to them, they did not believe them. 12 'II After these things he appeared to two of them in another

took counsel; and they gave money, not a small sum, to the guards, 13 Telling them, Say that his disciples came by night and stole him while we were sleeping. 14 And if this should be heard by the governor, we will appeal to him and declare that you are blameless. 15 So they took the money and did as they were instructed; and this word went out among the Jews, even to this day. 16 The eleven disciples then went to Galilee to a mountain where Jesus had promised to meet them. 17 And when they saw him, they worshipped him; but some of them were doubtful.

18 And Jesus came up and spoke with them, and said to them, All power in heaven and on earth has been given to me. Just as my Father has sent me I am also sending you.

manner, as they were walking and going to a village. 13 And they went and told the rest; but they did not believe them also.

14 At last he appeared to the eleven while they were reclining, and he upbraided them for their little faith and the dullness of their hearts, because they had not believed those who saw him risen. 15 And he said to them, Go into all the world and preach my gospel to the Whole creation. 16 He who believes and is baptized shall be saved; and he who does not believe shall be condemned. 17 And wonders will follow those who believe these things. In my name they will cast out demons; and they will speak with new tongues;

18 And they will handle snakes; [Aramaic idiom for enemies.] and if they should drink any poison of death, it will not harm them; and they

19 Go, therefore, and convert all nations; and baptize them in the name of the Father and of the Son and of the Holy Spirit;

20 And teach them to obey everything that I have commanded you; and, lo, I am with you all the days, to the end of the world. Amen.

will lay their hands on the sick, and they will be healed.

19 Then our Lord Jesus, after he had spoken to them, ascended to heaven and sat on the right hand of God. 20 And they went out and preached in every place; and our Lord helped them and strengthened their words by the miracles which they performed'

There came a moment, just before Jesus ascended, when he gathered his followers and issued a final, focused instruction:

"Do not leave Jerusalem, but wait for the gift my Father promised, which you have heard me speak about. For John baptized with water, but in a few days you will be baptized with the Holy Spirit."

—*Acts 1:4–5*

This was not merely a pause in the story. It was the calm before the creative storm. Jesus was not asking them to prepare a program, draft a mission strategy, or replicate his miracles. He was calling them to wait—to stand still until God moved. For what was coming was not something they could manufacture. It was not a reward for piety or an upgrade in personal experience. It was the promised gift of the Father, spoken of in ancient prophecy, and affirmed in Jesus' own teaching. It was the outpouring of God's own Spirit, the marker that the age to come was breaking into the present.

And when it came—on the day of Pentecost—it was unmistakable. Flames like fire. A rushing wind. Languages spoken and understood by people from every corner of the empire. The watching crowd was bewildered. Some mocked. "They're drunk," they said. But Peter, standing in the power of what had just come upon him, declared:

> *"These men are not drunk, as you suppose. It's only nine in the morning! No, this is what was spoken by the prophet Joel..."*
>
> —*Acts 2:15–16*

Here is the critical point: this moment was not the birth of a new spiritual technique, nor the introduction of a new religious ritual. It was the fulfillment of prophecy, the arrival of God's long-promised presence to dwell within his people. The Spirit had been spoken of by Joel, echoed through Isaiah and Ezekiel, and promised by Jesus himself. And now, in this dramatic and unrepeatable act of divine self-giving, the church was born—not by human planning, but by divine initiative.

It is vital to understand: Pentecost is not a command. It is a gift, a sovereign act of God inaugurating a new era. It is not something the disciples accomplished by their effort, nor something the church is told to recreate. We are not called to chase the event, but to live in its power.

To confuse the moment of Pentecost with a command to be repeated is to miss the point entirely. Just as Israel did not repeat the crossing of the Red Sea or re-enact the giving of the Law on Sinai, so too the church does not re-stage Pentecost. It was a decisive moment—a line drawn in salvation history.

The baptism of the Holy Spirit, then, is not a formula to be applied, but a promise fulfilled. It marked the shift from waiting to witnessing, from anticipation to mission. And from that moment forward, every man and woman who comes to faith in Jesus does so by the Spirit's power, is drawn into the life of the Spirit, and is equipped to bear witness to the risen Lord.

Our call today is not to replicate Pentecost—but to live as its result, as Spirit-filled people bearing the gospel to the ends of the earth, just as Jesus commanded.

There is a singular moment in the story of God's purposes when heaven itself broke into history with unmistakable clarity—and it happened, not in a temple, but in an upper room filled with ordinary Galileans.

These were men of no particular reputation—fishermen, tradesmen, provincial folk from the north of Israel who spoke only Aramaic. Yet on that day, the baptism of the Holy Spirit came not as a whisper of private spirituality, but as a public, world-shaking event. As tongues of fire rested upon them, they began to speak—not in the tongue of Galilee, but in the languages of the nations.

> "Now there were staying in Jerusalem God-fearing Jews from every nation under heaven. When they heard this sound, a crowd came together in bewilderment, because each one heard them speaking in his own language. Utterly amazed, they asked: 'Are not all these men who are speaking Galileans? Then how is it that each of us hears them in his own native language?'"
>
> —Acts 2:5–8

This was not confusion. It was divine clarity. What had been divided at Babel was being reversed at Pentecost. The fragmentation of language and culture that marked the scattering of humanity was now being drawn together—not by empire, not by power, but by the Spirit of the risen Messiah. The gospel was already going out to the world, and it was doing so in the native tongues of its hearers.

This, then, is the uniqueness of the baptism of the Holy Spirit at Pentecost. It was not simply an experience for the apostles; it was the inauguration of the church, the beginning of God's kingdom breaking forth on earth, as Jesus had promised. The outpouring of the Spirit was the signal that the age to come had arrived, that the new covenant people of God—Jew and Gentile alike—would now be formed, not by ancestry or temple ritual, but by faith in the crucified and risen Jesus, empowered by the very Spirit of God.

To confuse this moment with a pattern to be ritualized or repeated is to miss its narrative weight. Pentecost is not an individual benchmark but a historical turning point. It was never meant to be replicated—it was meant to launch the mission of the church.

In this sense, the Spirit's work at Pentecost is not normative in form, but normative in purpose. The tongues of fire, the foreign languages, the gathered nations—these were signs that the gospel was for all, and that the people of God were now a missionary people, sent not with swords or political agendas, but with good news in the power of the Spirit.

The church does not live by seeking another Pentecost. The church lives because Pentecost has already happened. The kingdom of God has come, the King has ascended, and the Spirit has been poured out. Our calling now is to bear witness—to go into all the world, speaking in every language the world understands, embodying the gospel of reconciliation and hope.

This is the power of Pentecost. And it remains the foundation of who we are.

Conversions in the First Church

We must begin by recognizing the extraordinary scale and immediacy of what unfolded after Peter's Spirit-empowered proclamation on the day of Pentecost. This was not the beginning of a new religion in the modern sense. It was, rather, the fulfillment of Israel's story—a moment when the ancient promises of God collided with the present reality of the crucified and risen Messiah.

> *"Therefore, let all Israel be assured of this: God has made this Jesus, whom you crucified, both Lord and Christ."*
>
> *—Acts 2:36*

The gravity of Peter's words was not lost on his hearers. This wasn't a theoretical reflection or a gentle invitation—it was a prophetic indictment followed by a call to covenant renewal. The Messiah had come, and they had rejected him. But the good news—the astonishing news—was that even now, the door to salvation stood open.

Luke tells us that the people were "cut to the heart." This is the work of the Spirit, not merely producing emotion but leading to repentance, that decisive reorientation of life away from sin and toward the living God.

> *"Brothers, what shall we do?" they asked.*

> *And Peter replied:*

"Repent and be baptized, every one of you, in the name of Jesus the Christ, for the forgiveness of your sins. And you will receive the gift of the Holy Spirit."

—Acts 2:37–38

Here, we see the pattern of conversion that defines the early church:

- Repentance—a turning from the old way of life, a recognition that one's assumptions about God and the world must be reshaped around Jesus.
- Baptism—a public act of identification with the Messiah and his new community.
- Forgiveness—not just a wiping away of past sins, but an entrance into the restored relationship with God promised by the prophets.
- The Holy Spirit—the presence of God dwelling not in a temple of stone, but in a renewed people.

"This promise," Peter continues, "is for you and your children and for all who are far off—for all whom the Lord our God will call."

This is the mission of the church in embryo. The gospel was not a private message to be savored in solitude, but a kingdom announcement meant to reshape whole communities. The call to "save yourselves from this corrupt generation" was not escapism, but an urgent summons to live as God's new creation in the midst of a broken world.

And the result?

> *"Those who accepted his message were baptized, and about three thousand were added to their number that day."*
>
> —*Acts 2:41*

This was not a crowd merely swayed by rhetoric. These were people who joined the new movement—people who recognized in Jesus the fulfillment of Israel's story, and who now gave themselves wholly to the life of this new people.

Luke paints a picture of their life together:

> *"They devoted themselves to the apostles' teaching and to fellowship, to the breaking of bread and to prayer."*
>
> —*Acts 2:42*

This is not casual participation. This is koinonia—a fellowship rooted in shared identity, shared resources, shared worship, and shared mission. The church was not a retreat from the world; it was the launch site of new creation. These first believers were the first outposts of God's kingdom, living under the reign of the risen Lord, empowered by the Holy Spirit.

The conversion of 3,000 souls in a single day was not the result of manipulation or mass emotion. It was the result of Spirit-empowered truth, proclaimed in the name of the crucified and risen Jesus, and received by hearts ready to be transformed.

This is how the church was born—not by coercion, but by conviction.

Not by tradition, but by truth.

Not by human ambition, but by the power of the Spirit.

And so, the question still echoes across time and space:

What shall we do?

And the answer remains the same:

Repent. Be baptized. Receive the gift. Join the story.

2) The Samaritans Believed and Were Baptized

(Acts 8:5–22)

As the gospel moved beyond Jerusalem, the next frontier was not the ends of the earth—but the fractured middle ground of Samaria. This was not a neutral mission field; it was enemy territory, so to speak—populated by a people long estranged from Jewish identity and worship, but still claiming Abrahamic roots. And yet, in the wisdom of God, Samaria was next.

Philip, one of the Seven, went down to a Samaritan city and proclaimed the Messiah, the Christ. This was no generic preaching—it was the proclamation that the long-awaited King of Israel had come, had died, had risen, and now reigned. And the signs followed. The afflicted were healed. The tormented were set free. The city, long captivated by false power, now tasted the true power of the kingdom of God. And the result?

"There was great joy in that city."

—*Acts 8:8*

Before this moment, the people had followed a man named Simon—a sorcerer, a manipulator, one who bewitched the people through spectacle. They called him "the Great Power of God"—but it was all a deception. Power without love. Signs without truth. But when Philip preached Christ, their allegiance shifted.

> "When they believed Philip as he proclaimed the good news of the kingdom of God and the name of Jesus Christ, they were baptized, both men and women."
>
> —Acts 8:12

Here is the significance: the gospel crossed a boundary that had stood for centuries. It reached into a people on the margins, and instead of asking them to become Jewish in form, it called them directly into the kingdom by faith and baptism. Even Simon—the deceiver himself—believed and was baptized. But as Luke will show, baptism is not the end of the journey. The heart still must be surrendered.

News of the Samaritan breakthrough reached Jerusalem. And so Peter and John were sent—not to correct Philip, but to confirm that the Spirit had indeed moved. But something unexpected occurred: although the Samaritans had believed and been baptized, the Holy Spirit had not yet come upon them.

> "Then they laid their hands on them, and they received the Holy Spirit."
>
> —Acts 8:17

This moment is not a prescription for all future conversions, but a unique turning point in salvation history. The apostles themselves had to witness the inclusion of Samaria. The rift between Jew and Samaritan was so deep that the Spirit chose to fall only when the apostles laid hands—not to deny the Samaritan faith, but to confirm to the apostles and the wider church that these "outsiders" were now fully included in the covenant people of God.

But Simon, ever the opportunist, misunderstood what was happening.

> *"When Simon saw that the Spirit was given through the laying on of the apostles' hands, he offered them money..."*
>
> —Acts 8:18

He saw the power, but not the grace. He saw the external sign, but missed the inner transformation. And so Peter, the same Peter who had once denied Christ but now stood filled with the Spirit, responded with apostolic severity:

> *"Let your silver perish with you, because you thought you could obtain the gift of God with money! You have no part or share in this ministry, because your heart is not right before God. Repent of this wickedness of yours..."*
>
> —Acts 8:20–22

Simon believed, yes. He was baptized, yes. But his heart remained unchanged. His story stands as a warning: true conversion is not merely external—it must penetrate to the very core of one's desires, motives, and loyalties. The gospel cannot be commodified. The Holy Spirit cannot be bought. The kingdom does not advance through manipulation, but through repentance, faith, and humble obedience.

In Samaria, then, we see the gospel tearing down centuries of division and prejudice—and building in its place a new humanity, formed by the Spirit, centered on the risen Christ.

3) The Ethiopian Eunuch Believed and Was Baptized

(Acts 8:25–39)

The gospel was on the move—not as a random sequence of spiritual encounters, but as a carefully orchestrated unfolding of God's redemptive plan. The risen Jesus had told his disciples that they would be his witnesses "in Jerusalem, Judea, Samaria, and to the ends of the earth." And now, with Jerusalem stirred and Samaria awakened, the next horizon beckoned.

As Peter and John returned from preaching through Samaritan villages, Philip—already proven faithful in frontier mission—was redirected by the angel of the Lord to a desert road stretching south from Jerusalem to Gaza. It was a strange instruction. No audience. No city. No visible mission field. Yet Philip obeyed.

And there, on that dry and dusty road, the next chapter in the story of the kingdom of God unfolded.

He encountered a eunuch from Ethiopia—a court official under Candace, queen of the Ethiopians, responsible for managing her treasure. This man was wealthy, educated, and—significantly—a God-fearer who had come to Jerusalem to worship. He was returning home, seated in his chariot, reading from the scroll of Isaiah.

Here is the remarkable thing: the Spirit of God was not only guiding Philip—He was already preparing the eunuch's heart, orchestrating a divine intersection of Scripture, longing, and gospel proclamation.

Philip heard him reading aloud—a common practice in the ancient world—and asked gently, "Do you understand what you are reading?" And the eunuch replied with a question that echoes the cry of the nations: "How can I, unless someone explains it to me?" (Acts 8:30–31)

He was reading Isaiah 53:

> *"He was led like a lamb to the slaughter... In his humiliation he was deprived of justice... Who can speak of his descendants? For his life was taken from the earth."*
>
> —Isaiah 53:7–8

This text, long cherished by Israel, had always stood as a mystery. Was Isaiah speaking of himself? Of another? Of Israel? The eunuch asked the most pivotal question: "Of whom does the prophet say this?"

> *"Then Philip opened his mouth and, beginning with that very Scripture, told him the good news about Jesus."*
>
> —Acts 8:35

Here, again, we see the shape of early evangelism. It was not a presentation of abstract doctrines—it was the unveiling of Jesus as the fulfillment of Israel's story, the one who suffered in innocence, who bore the sins of many, and who now reigns as Messiah and Lord.

And as the chariot rolled on, they came upon water. The eunuch, his heart ignited by the Word, asked the only question that remained:

> *"Look, here is water. What prevents me from being baptized?"*
>
> *—Acts 8:36*

It is a question filled with history and hope. As a eunuch, he would have been excluded from full participation in temple worship under the Mosaic law (see Deuteronomy 23:1). But in Jesus, all exclusions are overturned. In Jesus, the outsider is welcomed, the marginalized is embraced, and the boundaries of the people of God are redefined.

> *Philip said, "If you believe with all your heart, you may."*
>
> *And he replied, "I believe that Jesus Christ is the Son of God."*
>
> *—Acts 8:37*

And so they stopped the chariot. Both went down into the water. And the eunuch was baptized, just as Jesus had instructed: belief, confession, immersion—into Christ and into the new covenant family.

And then, in a moment both mysterious and Spirit-filled, Philip was taken away, and the eunuch continued on his journey rejoicing—a foretaste of how the gospel would reach the ends of the earth, long before Paul ever set foot in Europe.

This was not merely the conversion of an individual. It was the first recorded Gentile baptism. A royal official from Africa, a man marked by exclusion, became the first-fruit of a global mission. Isaiah's scroll had not only foretold the Suffering Servant—it had also envisioned a day when eunuchs and foreigners would be gathered into God's house (Isaiah 56:3–7). That day had arrived.

The gospel was not bound to geography, race, or ritual. It was—and is—a kingdom for all who believe, who listen, who follow.

4) Paul Believed and Was Baptized After Three Days of Prayer and Fasting

(Acts 9:3–20; Acts 22:16)

No single conversion in the New Testament is as startling, as public, or as theologically charged as that of Saul of Tarsus—the zealous persecutor turned apostle, the hunter of Christians who would become the greatest proclaimer of Christ.

Saul was not seeking Jesus; he was seeking to destroy the very movement that bore his name. He was armed with letters from the high priests, intending to arrest any who followed "The Way." But as he approached Damascus, a light from heaven interrupted his mission—and everything changed.

> *"Saul, Saul, why do you persecute me? It is hard for you to kick against the goads."*
>
> —Acts 9:4–5

Here we see the risen Lord himself confronting Saul, not with vengeance, but with a question—one that reveals the deep identification Jesus has with his people: "Why do you persecute me?" To attack the church is to strike at Christ himself.

Blinded, bewildered, and humbled, Saul is led into Damascus. For three days, he neither eats nor drinks. This was no mere physical reaction—it was a season of soul-deep undoing, of prayer and repentance. Saul had seen the Lord. His old worldview was collapsing, and something entirely new was beginning to emerge.

Meanwhile, the Lord was preparing a man named Ananias—a disciple in Damascus. Understandably hesitant, Ananias reminded God of Saul's violent reputation. But the Lord replied with words that would echo through church history:

> *"Go, for he is a chosen instrument of mine to carry my name before Gentiles, kings, and the children of Israel."*
>
> *—Acts 9:15*

And so Ananias went. He entered the house, laid his hands on Saul, and spoke with the language of grace:

> *"Brother Saul, the Lord Jesus who appeared to you has sent me so that you may regain your sight and be filled with the Holy Spirit."*
>
> *—Acts 9:17*

At that moment, something like scales fell from Saul's eyes. The man who had been blind in more ways than one could now see—both physically and spiritually. And what did he do next?

> *"He arose and was baptized."*
>
> *—Acts 9:18*

He did not delay. The man who had fiercely opposed the name of Jesus now obeyed the command of Jesus to repent, be baptized, and enter into the very community he once tried to destroy. He broke his fast, received strength, and stayed with the believers—no longer as enemy, but as brother.

And almost immediately, Saul began to proclaim Jesus in the synagogues:

> *"He is the Son of God."*
>
> —Acts 9:20

This was no gradual ideological shift. It was a complete transformation. Saul the Pharisee became Paul the apostle, not because he discovered a new religion, but because the risen Jesus confronted him, claimed him, forgave him, and commissioned him.

Years later, in his own testimony before a hostile audience in Jerusalem, Paul would recount the moment with striking clarity:

> *"And now, why do you delay? Arise, and be baptized, and wash away your sins, calling on the name of the Lord."*
>
> —Acts 22:16

This was not poetic language—it was obedience to the command of Christ. Paul knew that forgiveness, new life, and entrance into God's family were not vague spiritual ideas—they came through turning, believing, being baptized, and calling on the name of Jesus.

And so we see again: whether in Jerusalem, Samaria, Ethiopia, or Damascus, the call is consistent—the same message the risen Jesus gave before his ascension:

"Make disciples of all nations, baptizing them... teaching them to obey everything I have commanded you." (Matthew 28:19–20)

Paul obeyed. And the world was never the same.

5) Cornelius Believed and Was Baptized, According to Jesus' Instruction

(Acts 10:1–48; 11:5–18; 15:1–10)

If Pentecost marked the day the Spirit descended upon devout Jews in Jerusalem, then the house of Cornelius marks the day the kingdom of God broke fully into Gentile territory—and the message of Jesus Christ extended to "all nations," just as he had promised.

Cornelius was a man who lived with integrity. A Roman centurion stationed in Caesarea, part of the occupying imperial force, and yet also a God-fearer—a Gentile who worshiped the God of Israel, gave generously to the poor, and prayed faithfully. He was, by every outward measure, a good and devout man. But being righteous is not the same as being saved.

And God made that distinction clear.

> *"Your prayers and alms have ascended as a memorial before God. Now send men to Joppa and bring one Simon, who is called Peter."*
>
> —*Acts 10:4–5*

Though Cornelius prayed, though he gave, though he revered the God of Israel, salvation still required hearing the gospel, believing in Jesus, and being baptized. Not even an angel could deliver this message—for the proclamation of the gospel is entrusted not to heavenly beings, but to human witnesses who themselves have been transformed by grace.

At the same time, Peter, the apostle to the Jews, was receiving a vision of his own—a sheet lowered from heaven filled with animals considered unclean. The Lord was preparing Peter to see that what once divided Jew and Gentile no longer defined God's people. The old boundary markers were being redrawn, not around ethnicity or ritual purity, but around faith in Jesus the Messiah.

And so Peter came to Cornelius's house—reluctantly at first, but obediently. There, he found something remarkable: an entire household gathered in faith, waiting to hear what God had to say.

> *"Now we are all here in the presence of God to listen to everything the Lord has commanded you to tell us."*
>
> —*Acts 10:33*

Peter began to preach—not a new religion, but the fulfillment of Israel's story in Jesus of Nazareth. He told of Jesus' anointing with the Holy Spirit and power, his ministry of healing and freedom, his death by crucifixion, and his resurrection from the dead. And then, the great declaration:

> *"Everyone who believes in him receives forgiveness of sins through his name."*
>
> —*Acts 10:43*

And then—as Peter was still speaking—something unexpected, and yet divinely familiar, took place:

> *"The Holy Spirit fell on all who heard the word."*
>
> —Acts 10:44

Just as it had happened in Jerusalem, it now happened in Caesarea. Gentiles—unbaptized, uncircumcised, unreformed—received the Spirit of God. The Jewish believers who came with Peter were astonished. How could this be?

But Peter saw clearly what God was doing. The Spirit had made no distinction.

> *"Can anyone withhold water for baptizing these people who have received the Holy Spirit just as we have?"*
>
> —Acts 10:47

And so he commanded them to be baptized in the name of the Lord Jesus. Not simply as a response to a private experience, but as full entry into the body of Christ, the covenant people of God, and the story of new creation.

Later, when questioned about this radical inclusion, Peter gave this defense:

> *"If then God gave the same gift to them as he gave to us when we believed in the Lord Jesus Christ, who was I that I could stand in God's way?"*
>
> —Acts 11:17

And at the Jerusalem Council, Peter would double down:

"God made no distinction between us and them, for he purified their hearts by faith."

—*Acts 15:9*

Cornelius and his household were not saved by visions, by morality, or by religious performance. They were saved because they heard the gospel, believed it, and obeyed the instruction of Jesus: "Whoever believes and is baptized will be saved." (Mark 16:16)

This is faith, the kind that sees the messenger, hears the message, and responds in obedience. It is the same kind of faith that Naaman had to learn through the wisdom of a servant girl in his household: that salvation comes not on our terms, but on God's.

In Cornelius, the gospel touched Rome. In his household, the nations began to gather. What God began with Israel, he was now accomplishing for the world.

6) Lydia Believed and Was Baptized, According to Jesus' Instruction

(Acts 16:13–15)

As the gospel swept outward from Jerusalem to Judea, to Samaria, and into Gentile lands, it eventually reached Europe—and when it did, it did not begin in palaces or public squares, but by a riverbank, in a quiet prayer gathering, outside the walls of a Roman colony called Philippi.

Paul, Silas, and their companions had been divinely redirected. The Spirit had prevented them from preaching in Asia, and then in Bithynia. Then came the vision—a Macedonian man pleading,

"Come over and help us." It was clear: God was opening Europe, and Philippi would be the doorway.

Yet there was no synagogue in Philippi, a sign that the Jewish population was likely small. And so, on the Sabbath, Paul and his team went outside the city gate to a place of prayer near the river, where a group of women had gathered.

> *"And we sat down and spoke to the women who had gathered there."*
>
> —Acts 16:13

Among them was Lydia, a businesswoman from Thyatira, a city known for its dyeing industry. She was a "seller of purple"—an entrepreneur dealing in luxury goods, yet also described as a worshiper of God. She was likely a Gentile who had come to revere the God of Israel, much like Cornelius before her.

But it was not her religious disposition that brought about her transformation. It was God's initiative.

> *"The Lord opened her heart to respond to Paul's message."*
>
> —Acts 16:14

Here is the beautiful mystery of grace: the gospel is proclaimed, but it is the Lord who opens hearts. Paul spoke of Jesus—the crucified and risen Messiah, the fulfillment of Israel's hope, the Savior of the world—and Lydia listened. She did not simply hear; she responded.

And how did she respond?

> *"She was baptized, along with her household."*

—*Acts 16:15*

In accordance with Jesus' instruction, Lydia believed and was baptized. Not as a private spiritual act, but as public identification with Jesus, a declaration that she now belonged to the Messiah's people, the new covenant family formed by grace and faith.

Lydia's response didn't end at the water's edge. She immediately expressed the fruit of her faith—hospitality, generosity, and partnership in the mission:

> *"If you judge me to be a true believer in the Lord, come and stay in my house."*

—*Acts 16:15*

So insistent was her invitation that the apostles accepted. Lydia's home became the first house church in Philippi, and possibly the first in all of Europe. She was, in every sense, a founding member of the church—a woman of means, of faith, and of courage.

Her conversion reminds us that the advance of the kingdom is not always loud or dramatic. Sometimes, it happens in quiet places, among faithful women, through a simple conversation beside a river. And yet, it is no less powerful. It is the same gospel, the same instruction of Jesus, and the same Spirit at work—opening hearts, forming new communities, and changing the world one life at a time.

7) The Jailer Believed and Was Baptized, According to Jesus' Instruction

(Acts 16:16–36)

The gospel has never advanced without resistance. As Paul and Silas proclaimed Jesus in Philippi, casting out a spirit of divination from a young enslaved woman, they struck at the heart of both economic exploitation and spiritual deception. The result? Not a celebration, but a riot.

Dragged before the authorities, stripped, beaten, and thrown into the deepest part of the prison, Paul and Silas suffered not for breaking laws, but for breaking chains—both spiritual and social.

But even a prison cell could not silence the gospel.

> *"Around midnight, Paul and Silas were praying and singing hymns to God, and the other prisoners were listening to them."*
>
> —Acts 16:25

This was not mere endurance. This was worship in the face of injustice, a testimony that even in suffering, the Lord reigns.

Then came the earthquake—not just geological, but theological. The prison shook, the doors burst open, the chains fell off. And yet, no one ran. This wasn't a jailbreak—it was a divine appointment.

The jailer, waking to the scene, assumed the worst. In Roman law, a guard who lost his prisoners faced execution. Despairing, he drew his sword to take his own life. But then came the voice that would change everything:

> *"Do not harm yourself, for we are all here."*
>
> —Acts 16:28

Paul's words stopped the blade. And in that moment, something deeper shook the jailer—not the ground, but his soul. He rushed in, trembling, and fell at the feet of the prisoners he had once chained.

> *"Sirs, what must I do to be saved?"*
>
> —Acts 16:30

This is the question that echoes across Acts. And the answer remains the same:

> *"Believe in the Lord Jesus, and you will be saved—you and your household."*
>
> —Acts 16:31

But belief is never merely mental assent. As always in the New Testament, belief is relational trust and covenant response—a turning of the whole self toward Jesus, expressed in action.

Paul and Silas preached the word of the Lord to him and to everyone in his household. And in the middle of the night, the jailer washed their wounds—a gesture of repentance, of humility, and perhaps of gratitude.

Then, in that same hour, he and his household were baptized. Not after a long catechism. Not after religious ritual. But in response to the gospel—in obedience to Jesus' own words: "Whoever believes and is baptized will be saved." (Mark 16:16)

> *"And he brought them into his house and set a meal before them. He and his entire household rejoiced, because they had come to believe in God."* —Acts 16:34

What began with suffering in a prison ended in joy in a home. The gospel had once again crossed boundaries—geographic, social, institutional—and found a place in the heart of a Roman jailer. His household, once guarded by violence, was now marked by grace, table fellowship, and new life in Christ.

Here we see, once again, the consistent pattern of the early church: preaching, believing, baptism, rejoicing. And not just individuals, but households—entire communities brought under the lordship of Jesus.

Even in the darkest of places—even in the watchtowers of empire—the light of Christ breaks in. And those who receive him, like the jailer, are never the same.

8) Crispus and His Household Believed and Were Baptized, According to Jesus' Instruction

(Acts 18:1–11)

When Paul arrived in Corinth, the bustling Roman port city where trade, philosophy, idolatry, and skepticism intertwined, he did not begin with spectacle, but with fellowship and faithfulness. He found Aquila and Priscilla—exiles from Rome—and joined them in their tentmaking trade. Yet even as he worked with his hands, Paul's heart and voice were fixed on the mission entrusted to him: to proclaim Jesus as the Christ.

"He reasoned in the synagogue every Sabbath, trying to persuade both Jews and Greeks."
—Acts 18:4

But when resistance arose, Paul didn't withdraw in defeat—he pivoted in obedience. With garments shaken and words of warning, he turned to the Gentiles, entering the home of Titius Justus, a Gentile God-fearer who lived right next to the synagogue.

And then something remarkable happened.

"Crispus, the synagogue leader, believed in the Lord—together with his entire household. And many of the Corinthians who heard Paul believed and were baptized." —Acts 18:8

Crispus, a man of stature in the Jewish community, did not allow his status to block the movement of grace. He heard the gospel, he believed, and he obeyed Jesus' instruction—he was baptized, publicly identifying with Christ. Not only that, but his entire household followed, marking another crucial moment in the spread of the gospel to households, not just individuals.

And the floodgates opened. Many in Corinth believed and were baptized, not because they were persuaded by signs alone, but because the Spirit of God was calling them, and they responded in faith.

Paul would remain in Corinth for eighteen months, teaching the word of God and strengthening the young church. It was not the cultural elite or the religiously powerful who received the kingdom—it was those who, like Crispus, heard and obeyed.

9) Disciples in Ephesus Were Re-baptized and Received the Holy Spirit, According to Jesus' Instruction

Then Paul came to Ephesus, another cosmopolitan hub filled with philosophical inquiry, spiritual hunger, and syncretistic confusion.

There, he encountered a group of disciples—men who, at first glance, appeared sincere and devout. But something was missing.

"Did you receive the Holy Spirit when you believed?" Paul asked. "We have not even heard that there is a Holy Spirit," they replied.*
—*Acts 19:2*

This exchange reveals a deeper truth: sincerity alone does not equal salvation. These men had received John's baptism—a baptism of repentance, of preparation. But John himself had always pointed forward, to the One who would baptize with the Holy Spirit and fire.

"John baptized with a baptism of repentance," Paul said, "telling the people to believe in the one who was to come after him—that is, in Jesus." —*Acts 19:4*

And when they heard this, they didn't argue or delay. They obeyed. They were baptized—not again in form, but now in the name of the Lord Jesus (v.5). And then Paul laid hands on them, and the Holy Spirit came upon them, with manifestations of tongues and prophecy—just as at Pentecost.

Why this pattern?

Your insight is deeply perceptive: these were men whose previous baptism might have appeared externally similar, yet lacked the inward fulfillment. John's baptism prepared the heart, but only Jesus' baptism grants forgiveness, indwelling, and full inclusion into the new covenant community. The laying on of hands and the visible giving of the Spirit served as divine confirmation—not of ritual, but of the reality that this was different, and now complete.

Just as with Cornelius, the Spirit acted in ways that confirmed the gospel's reach and depth. It was not about duplicating events, but about making clear that salvation comes only through the name of Jesus, in obedience to his word.

Obedience: The Line that Divides

In all these stories—from Pentecost to Ephesus—there is one clear thread: obedience to Jesus' instruction. Not partial belief. Not religious identity. Not inherited morality. But a living, active, courageous obedience that mirrors the faith of Naaman, who had to be humbled in order to be healed, and of Paul, who had to lose everything in order to gain Christ.

As Jesus himself declared:

"Not everyone who says to me, 'Lord, Lord,' will enter the kingdom of heaven, but only the one who does the will of my Father who is in heaven." —Matthew 7:21

To hear and not obey is to build on sand. To obey, even when others resist, even when it costs everything, is to build on the rock.

The first-century believers—from Jerusalem to Judea, from Samaria to the ends of the earth—did not craft their own terms of discipleship. They believed, repented, and were baptized, just as Jesus commanded. The evidence of true faith was never emotion alone, or even miracles, but a heart made willing, and a life reordered around the lordship of Christ.

The call remains. The instruction has not changed.

Interpret the Lord's command at your own peril. Obey it—and live.

6

Paul and the troubled waters

Up to this point, the narrative of Scripture has unfolded with deliberate purpose. John the Baptist, the one foretold by the prophet Isaiah and echoing the spirit of Elijah, emerged from the wilderness calling Israel to repentance. He stood in the long prophetic tradition—yet his message was more than protest or warning. It was preparation. John's baptism was a summons to change: to realign one's life, to turn away from sin and await the one who would come after him, "whose sandals I am not worthy to untie."

Then came Jesus. Not in royal robes or armed rebellion, but as a Galilean carpenter, quietly submitting himself to John's baptism. At that moment—the waters of the Jordan stirred, the heavens were opened, and the Spirit of God descended like a dove, marking Jesus not merely as a prophet, but as the beloved Son. The voice from heaven confirmed what Israel had long awaited: here, at last, was the Messiah, and with him, the kingdom of God was arriving.

From that point on, Jesus called men and women to follow him, not in theory, but in life, in repentance, and through baptism into this new covenant reality.

But perhaps nowhere do we see the transforming power of that call more vividly than in the story of Saul of Tarsus.

Paul's Conversion: Obedience, Not Abstraction

Saul had built his identity upon zeal for the law, a fierce commitment to the traditions of his ancestors. He was no irreligious man—far from it. He believed he was serving God by persecuting those who followed the crucified Nazarene. But as he traveled to Damascus—commissioned by the religious authorities to arrest and punish disciples of Jesus—he encountered not a doctrine or a rumor, but the risen Christ himself.

"Saul, Saul, why do you persecute me?" —Acts 26:14

The voice was unmistakable. And when Saul asked "Who are you, Lord?", the answer shattered his assumptions:

"I am Jesus of Nazareth, whom you are persecuting."

This moment did not merely change Saul's direction—it redefined his identity. Blinded and bewildered, he spent three days in prayer and fasting. And then came Ananias, a simple disciple sent by the Lord with a mission: not to philosophize, but to deliver the instruction of Jesus.

"What are you waiting for? Arise and be baptized, and wash away your sins, calling on his name." —Acts 22:16

And Saul obeyed.

He repented.

He believed.

He was baptized.

And in that act of obedience, he was no longer Saul the persecutor, but Paul the apostle, sent not just to Israel, but to the nations—to kings and Gentiles, to philosophers and slaves, to proclaim the Jesus he once opposed.

Paul Before Kings: The Gospel Made Personal

Years later, now a prisoner, Paul stood before King Agrippa and gave one of the most powerful testimonies in the New Testament. He did not merely recite doctrine. He told his story. And he showed that everything he preached—repentance, faith, and obedience—was rooted in his own experience of grace:

> *He threw many of the saints (disciples of Christ as they were called) into prison, having received authority from the chief priests; and when some were put to death, I took part with those who condemned them.*
>
> *11 And I tortured them in every synagogue, thus compelling them to blaspheme the name of Jesus; and being exceedingly mad against them, I also went to other cities to persecuted them.*
>
> *12 I was on the way to Damascus for this purpose, with authority and commission from the chief priests, when,*
>
> *13 At midday on the road, O king, I saw a light from heaven more powerful than that of the sun, shining round about me and upon those who journeyed with me.*

14 When we all fell to the ground, then I heard a voice speaking to me, in the Hebrew tongue, Saul, Saul, why do you persecute me? It is hard for you to kick against the pricks.

15 And I said, My Lord, who are you? And our Lord said to me, I am Jesus of Nazareth whom you persecute.

16 Then he said to me, Rise and stand upon your feet; for I have appeared to you for this purpose, to appoint you a minister and a witness both of those things in which you have seen me and of those things in which you will also see me again. 17 And I will deliver you from the Jewish people and from the other peoples to Whom I send you, 18 To open their eyes, that they may turn from darkness to light and from the power of Satan to God and receive forgiveness of sins and a portion with the saints who are of the faith in me.

19 Where upon, O King Agrippa, I did not disobey the heavenly vision; 20 But I preached first to them of Damascus and at Jerusalem and throughout all the villages of Judea and then to the Gentiles, that they might repent and turn to God and do works worthy of repentance.

21 For these causes the Jews seized me in the temple and wanted to kill me.

22 But God has helped me to this very day, and behold I stand and testify to the humble and to the great, saying nothing contrary to Moses and the prophets, but the very things which they said were to take place,

23 That Christ should suffer and that he should be the first to rise from the dead and that he should preach light to the people and to the Gentiles. 24 And while Paul was pleading in this manner, Festus cried with a loud voice, Paul, you are overwrought. Much study has made you mad.

25 But Paul said to him, I am not mad, O most excellent Festus; but I speak the words of truth and soberness.

26 And King Agrippa is also familiar with these things, and this is why I am speaking openly before him, because I think not one of these words has been hidden from him; for they were not done in secret.

27 King Agrippa, do you believe the prophets? I know that you believe.

28 Then King Agrippa said to him, With little effort you almost persuade me to become a Christian.

29 And Paul said, I pray God that not only you, but also all of those who hear me today were as I am, except for these bonds.

"I was not disobedient to the heavenly vision... I preached that people should repent, turn to God, and do works worthy of repentance." —Acts 26:19-20

Though Agrippa famously replied, "You almost persuade me to become a Christian," the gospel had once again been faithfully proclaimed. Paul did not compromise. He pointed to the suffering and resurrection of the Messiah, and the light made available to all—Jew and Gentile alike.

Obedience: The Test of True Faith

Paul's life illustrates a vital truth: the question "What must I do to be saved?" finds its answer not in speculation, but in obedience to the command of Jesus. That same pattern—repentance, faith, baptism—is repeated throughout Acts. Whether a devout Ethiopian, a Roman centurion, a wealthy woman in Philippi, or a hardened jailer in the middle of the night, the response is the same: hear the gospel, believe, and obey.

Even Paul's own theology points back to this. In his letter to the Romans, he explains that through baptism we are buried with Christ and raised with him, that we might walk in newness of life (Romans 6:3-4). Baptism, for Paul, was never a symbol only—it was the entry point into God's new world, a world reoriented around Jesus as Lord.

Naaman, Paul, and the Struggle to Obey

Here we see a parallel that echoes through Scripture: Naaman the Syrian was told to dip himself in a river to be cleansed. He nearly refused—not because the command was unclear, but because it seemed too simple, too humbling. It was a servant girl, a voice from the margins, who reminded him: "If the prophet had told you to do something great, would you not have done it?"

Likewise, Paul, the powerful Pharisee, had to humble himself—to be led blind, to receive the word from an ordinary man, and to go down into the waters of baptism.

The gospel calls us to obedience, not convenience. And this is where many stumble—not because the way is unclear, but because it requires surrender. Like the rich man who turned away sorrowfully from Jesus, we too wrestle with pride, self-sufficiency, and the illusion of control.

But the call remains, as clear as ever: "Repent and be baptized, every one of you... and you will receive the gift of the Holy Spirit." (Acts 2:38)

To Interpret or To Obey?

We live in a time much like the first century—full of ideas, philosophies, and religious interpretations. But the message of the gospel is not subject to reinterpretation. It is a call to decision. As Jesus warned:

"Not everyone who says to me, 'Lord, Lord,' will enter the kingdom of heaven, but only the one who does the will of my Father in heaven."
—Matthew 7:21

Obedience is the evidence of faith. Baptism is the mark of entry. And the path of salvation is not complicated—but it is costly, for it calls us to surrender everything.

Like Naaman, like Paul, like so many before and after, the question is not "Do we understand it fully?" but "Are we willing to trust and obey?"

To interpret the Lord's instruction is to risk shaping God in our image.

To obey it is to be shaped into the image of Christ.

The choice is yours.

Baptism, Resurrection, and the New Life in Christ

The apostle Peter, who first stood on the day of Pentecost and declared that everyone who repents and is baptized in the name of Jesus would receive the gift of the Holy Spirit, did not change his message with time. Writing later to the scattered believers in Asia Minor, he reminded them that baptism is not a mere ritual—it is a saving act, not because of what water does to the body, but because of what God does in the heart, through the resurrection of Jesus the Messiah.

"Christ suffered once for sins, the righteous for the unrighteous, to bring you to God. He was put to death in the flesh but made alive in the Spirit." —**1 Peter 3:18**

In this resurrection life, Peter says, Christ preaches even to the spirits held in bondage—to those who in Noah's day rejected the patience of God, even as the ark was being prepared. Only eight were saved through water, and Peter draws the line forward:

"This water symbolizes baptism that now saves you also—not the removal of dirt from the body, but the pledge of a clean conscience toward God. It saves you by the resurrection of Jesus Christ." —**1 Peter 3:21**

Baptism is not magic. It is not superstition. It is the turning point—the moment of new birth, where we are joined with the Messiah not only in name, but in death and resurrection. It is covenantal. Transformational. And it brings us under the authority of the risen Lord, who now sits at the right hand of God, with angels, authorities, and powers made subject to him (v.22).

And Paul, writing to the believers in Rome, clarifies this further with theological precision and pastoral urgency:

"Do you not know that all of us who were baptized into Christ Jesus were baptized into his death?" —**Romans 6:3**

This is not metaphor. It is participation. In baptism, we do not simply remember the death of Jesus—we enter it. We are buried with him, not in soil but in water, so that just as he was raised, we too are raised to walk in newness of life.

"For if we have been united with him in a death like his, we will certainly also be united with him in a resurrection like his." —**Romans 6:5**

Baptism, then, is not the end of something—it is the beginning. It is the dying of the old self, the crucifixion of sin's dominion, and the emergence of a new humanity, alive to God and empowered to live under the reign of grace.

Paul goes on to say:

"Our old self was crucified with him so that the body ruled by sin might be done away with... For the one who has died has been set free from sin." —**Romans 6:6–7**

This is liberation—not just from guilt, but from sin's enslaving power. And so, Paul calls the church to live into the reality that their baptism declares:

"Count yourselves dead to sin but alive to God in Christ Jesus. Therefore, do not let sin reign in your mortal body... but offer yourselves to God as those who have been brought from death to life." —**Romans 6:11–13**

This is what it means to be under grace, not law. Not lawlessness, but new creation. A new identity. A new allegiance.

The apostles are united in this: Peter and Paul both proclaim that baptism is the entrance into resurrection life, not by external ritual, but by internal transformation. It is the response of faith to the call of Christ. It is the obedient surrender of a heart being made new. And it is only through this surrender that sin loses its power and the reign of grace begins.

PAUL'S moment of decision

"What Is Wrong with How I've Been Living? What Is the Message? What Must I Do to Be Saved?"

At some point—perhaps many times in a lifetime—every human being comes to a moment of decision. It is not always dramatic or public. Sometimes, it comes quietly, through suffering or weariness, through disillusionment or longing. For others, it comes like a flash of lightning, as it did for Saul of Tarsus on the road to Damascus. But whenever it comes, it carries the same gravity: the confrontation of one's life with the message of Jesus.

And here is the message:

"God has made this Jesus, whom you crucified, both Lord and Messiah." —**Acts 2:36**

This message isn't simply religious advice. It is the declaration that God's kingdom has come, that Jesus is King, and that the old way of living—centered on self, sin, and independence—has come to an end. That way leads not to freedom, but to bondage and death. The world says "follow your heart," but Jesus says, "Deny yourself, take up your cross, and follow me."

This is why repentance is so vital. Repentance isn't self-loathing or moral perfectionism. It is a radical change of direction—a turning from sin, yes, but also a turning toward Jesus. It is not simply feeling sorry for doing wrong. It is choosing to live differently because you now see differently.

You ask, "What is wrong with how I've been living?"

And the answer, in simplest terms, is this: we've been living apart from God's reign. We've built lives—even religious ones—on our own terms. We've trusted in our own judgment, followed our own desires, and silenced our conscience when it cried out. We have sinned—some publicly, some privately—but all of us alike have fallen short of the glory of God.

"There is no one righteous, not even one." **—Romans 3:10**

But the gospel is not about guilt—it is about grace. And the good news is this:

"While we were still sinners, Christ died for us." **—Romans 5:8**

The message of Jesus is that a new world has begun, and you are invited to be part of it. But it begins with a death to the old self—not metaphorical only, but real and enacted through baptism. As Paul wrote:

"Do you not know that all of us who were baptized into Christ Jesus were baptized into his death?... So that just as Christ was raised from the dead, we too may walk in newness of life." **—Romans 6:3-4**

So what must you do to be saved?

Not work harder. Not become perfect. But this:

1. Hear the message of Jesus, not as theory but as truth.

2. Believe that he is who he claimed to be—Lord, Messiah, risen Son of God.

3. Repent—not in general, but in response to his call on your life. Acknowledge what your conscience already knows: the things in you that are killing you.

4. Be baptized in his name, entering into his death and resurrection.

5. Receive the Holy Spirit—the power to live this new life.

6. Live daily in obedience to the Lordship of Christ.

This is not a checklist—it is the pattern of surrender that reorients the entire self toward God.

And yes, as you rightly said: *"The truth is that without a realization of what one must repent from, one cannot even begin to repent."*

This is why the gospel must be preached—to bring every man and woman face to face with Jesus. We cannot repent from what we do not see. But once we see him—his mercy, his call, his sacrifice—we cannot remain the same.

"Today, if you hear his voice, do not harden your hearts." — **Hebrews 3:15**

This is your moment of decision.

Not to admire Jesus from a distance.

Not to reinterpret his words.

Not to delay.

But to say, like Paul:

"Lord, what shall I do?"

And to hear the answer echo back:

"Arise, and be baptized, and wash away your sins, calling on his name." —**Acts 22:16**

Paul and the Problem of Denominations

How Did We Get So Divided? A Word from Paul, and the Problem of Factionalism

It's one of the most perplexing realities of the Christian faith today: so many churches, so many doctrines, so many disagreements—denominations built not only around tradition or liturgy, but often around personal interpretation, personality, or preference.

But in the beginning, there was only one church. Not a monolith of uniformity, but a unified body held together by a single confession: Jesus is Lord.

Even in the first century, however, we see the seeds of factionalism taking root. The apostle Paul, who had traveled throughout the Mediterranean planting and strengthening churches, observed it firsthand—and his grief was palpable.

> *"I appeal to you, brothers and sisters, in the name of our Lord Jesus Christ, that all of you agree with one another... that there be no divisions among you, but that you be perfectly united in mind and thought."*
> **—1 Corinthians 1:10**

The concern was not theological curiosity, but allegiance to personalities. Some were saying, "I follow Paul." Others, "I follow Apollos." Still others, "I follow Peter." And perhaps most troubling, a group even claiming, "I follow Christ," as if to elevate themselves above the rest.

And Paul's rhetorical questions cut to the heart of it:

"Is Christ divided? Was Paul crucified for you? Were you baptized in the name of Paul?" — **1 Corinthians 1:13**

Apollos, Aquila, and the Problem of Incomplete Understanding

This concern didn't arise in a vacuum. Paul had seen firsthand how good intentions could still lead to partial understandings of the gospel. Take Apollos, for instance: an eloquent, powerful preacher from Alexandria who was fervent in spirit and well-versed in the Hebrew Scriptures. He preached about Jesus with zeal—but he only knew John's baptism.

"He began to speak boldly in the synagogue. When Priscilla and Aquila heard him, they invited him to their home and explained to him the way of God more accurately." — **Acts 18:26**

Apollos was sincere—but he was not yet complete in his understanding. He had passion, but lacked the full knowledge of Jesus' instruction regarding salvation—particularly baptism into the name of Jesus, and the giving of the Holy Spirit. And yet, rather than dismiss him, Priscilla and Aquila gently corrected him and brought him into deeper understanding. That act of love bore great fruit.

This very pattern repeated when Paul arrived in Ephesus and found a group of disciples who, like Apollos before, knew only the baptism of John. When Paul asked whether they had received the Holy Spirit, they replied that they had never even heard of it.

And so Paul responded not with judgment, but with truth.

"John's baptism was a baptism of repentance. He told the people to believe in the one coming after him, that is, in Jesus." —**Acts 19:4**

Upon hearing this, they were baptized in the name of the Lord Jesus, and when Paul laid hands on them, the Holy Spirit came upon them. Obedience to the message brought transformation.

Division: Then and Now

The early church's divisions did not stem from malice, but from immaturity, misunderstanding, and human pride. They were baptized into Jesus—but some began to place their trust in the messenger, rather than the message. And Paul, ever the pastor, sought to bring them back to the core:

"Christ did not send me to baptize, but to preach the gospel—not with eloquent wisdom, lest the cross of Christ be emptied of its power." —**1 Corinthians 1:17**

Even then, Paul knew that the power of the gospel would be undermined by allegiance to human leaders, or divisions based on personalities. And what began as minor fractures in the first century has, over time, become a kaleidoscope of denominations, often confusing, contradictory, and sometimes even hostile to one another.

But if Paul were among us today, he would surely ask again:

"Is Christ divided?"

The Path Back to Unity

The solution isn't organizational consolidation or institutional conformity. The solution is returning to the message of Jesus himself—the gospel of the kingdom, the call to repent, to believe, to be baptized into his name, and to be filled with his Spirit.

This unity is not about doctrine as data—but about being formed by one faith, one baptism, one Lord. It means humbling ourselves, as Apollos did, to be taught more accurately. It means choosing the cross over charisma, obedience over opinion.

"For the message of the cross is foolishness to those who are perishing, but to us who are being saved, it is the power of God."
—1 Corinthians 1:18

We need to recover the courage of Paul, the humility of Apollos, the gentleness of Priscilla and Aquila, and the single-minded focus of the early church: to know Christ, to proclaim Christ, and to obey Christ.

Not to follow Paul.

Not to follow Apollos.

Not to follow tradition or trend.

But to follow Jesus, crucified and risen, Lord and King.

Division and Worldliness: A Sign of Immaturity, Not of Christ

When Paul wrote to the Christians in Corinth, he wasn't writing to a strong, healthy, united church. He was writing to a divided and immature community, struggling with status, moral confusion, and spiritual one-upmanship. The Corinthians boasted in their leaders, compared their gifts, and flirted with the wisdom of the age—all while forgetting the scandalous simplicity of the cross and the obedient faith it requires.

Paul's language is sharp, but it is the severity of a loving parent correcting children:

"Brothers and sisters, I could not address you as spiritual but as worldly—as mere infants in Christ." **—1 Corinthians 3:1**

The problem wasn't that they lacked gifts or enthusiasm—it was that their hearts were still attached to the wrong things. They were acting like children, still preoccupied with status, division, jealousy, and quarrels. In today's terms, we might say they were drawn more to brand names, prosperity, and personality cults than to the sacrificial obedience of Jesus.

"One says, 'I follow Paul,' and another, 'I follow Apollos.' Are you not acting like mere humans?" **—1 Corinthians 3:4**

Paul doesn't rebuke them for following false teachers—Apollos, after all, was a faithful brother—but for treating ministers as if they were franchise owners of competing visions, rather than servants of the same Lord.

"I planted the seed, Apollos watered it, but God made it grow... Neither the one who plants nor the one who waters is anything, but only God, who makes things grow." **—1 Corinthians 3:6–7**

The church is not a human movement; it is the work of God's Spirit, and the moment we elevate personalities or programs above the message of Jesus, we are veering off course.

What Happened After the Apostles? The Tragic Path Toward Denomination

The early church, particularly in its first generations, was fiercely committed to one gospel, one Lord, one baptism. Wherever the apostles went—from Jerusalem to Antioch, from Ephesus to Rome—the message was Jesus is Lord, and the call was clear: repent, believe, be baptized, and follow him.

But as time passed, and especially from the 16th century onward, something changed. The Protestant Reformation, born out of a legitimate critique of corruption in the Roman Church, quickly fractured into multiple competing movements—each claiming to restore the gospel, but often sowing further division.

While reformers like Martin Luther challenged real abuses, the long-term outcome was a steady stream of new groups, each defining themselves by what they rejected, rather than by a shared obedience to the instruction of Jesus.

Since then, thousands of denominations have emerged. Some with minor differences, others with radical divergences from apostolic teaching. Some, like the Mormons or Jehovah's Witnesses, have gone so far as to rewrite the gospel itself, creating new books and systems of belief that pull people away from the foundation laid by Jesus and the apostles.

And perhaps most troubling: many of these religious movements flourished in Western cultures that also exported slavery, colonization, and cultural superiority—yet few of these denominations were known for standing prophetically against these evils. The irony is haunting. A church divided often becomes a church distracted—unable to bear witness to the justice and mercy of God.

Jesus Did Not Call You to a Denomination—He Called You to Obedience

Let us be absolutely clear: Jesus did not die to start a new religion or to inspire thousands of theological tribes. He came to establish God's kingdom, to call a people into covenant faithfulness, and to redeem the world through their obedience to him.

When you define your faith by a denomination—by Sabbath observance, speaking in tongues, or theological distinctives—you risk substituting identity in Christ with allegiance to tradition. These things may be part of your story, but they must never replace the core call to follow Jesus in truth.

"If you love me, keep my commandments." —**John 14:15**

The problem today is not simply that there are many churches. The problem is that many churches preach many gospels, creating confusion where there should be clarity, and allegiance to systems where there should be allegiance to Jesus Christ alone.

The Call Back to Unity and Simplicity in Christ

The apostolic witness calls us back—not to primitive Christianity as a cultural aesthetic, but to the radical unity of obedient faith. Unity does not mean sameness, but it does mean submission to the message of Jesus, and refusal to be divided by pride, preference, or personalities.

We must not follow Paul.

We must not follow Apollos.

We must not follow Luther, Calvin, Wesley, or Rome.

We must follow Jesus.

And we must do what he said:

"Go and make disciples of all nations, baptizing them... teaching them to obey everything I have commanded you." **—Matthew 28:19–20**

WHAT MUST I DO TO BE SAVED?

History of Major Denominations

Year	Denomination with differing doctrines	The Doctrinal Founder	Artifact
1517	Lutheranism	Martin Luther, Germany	Started reformation movement, Catholic
1523	Swiss Reformed Church	Huldrych Zwingli, Switzerland	Reformation preacher
1534	Anglican	King Henry 8th, England	King of England creates Church of England to approve his divorce
1536	Calvinism	John Calvin, Switzerland	Reformation Movement
1560	Presbyterianism	John Knox, Scotland	Reformation Movement
1605	Baptist Churches	John Smyth, Holland	Reformation Movement
1628	Dutch Reformed	Michaelis Jones, Netherlands	Reformation Movement
1647	Quakers	George Fox, England	English preacher
1693	Amish	Jakob Ammann, Switzerland	Anabaptists, Reformed Church
1744,	Methodism	John & Charles Wesley, England	Reformation Movement
1816	African Methodist	Richard Allen, Philadelphia	Formed a denomination for free black slaves
1820	Mormonism (Latter-day saints)	Joseph Smith, New York	The Book of Mormon
1832	Church of Christ	Alexander Campbell, W. Virginia, U.S.	Restoration Movement
1860	Seventh Day Adventists	Ellen White, W.Miller, NH, USA	Protestant, observance of Saturday sabbath
1865	Salvation Army	William Booth, England	Methodist, as a Christian charity organization
1870	Jehovah's Witnesses	Charles Russell, PA, USA	New World Translation (NWT), their own Bible
1879	Christian Science	Mary Baker Eddy, NH, USA	The Christian Science textbook
1890	Foursquare	Aimee McPherson, Ontario, Canada	Missionary preacher
1900	Pentecostalism	Charles Parham, J. Seymour, USA	American preacher, known for speaking in tongues
1933	Worldwide Church of God	Herbert W. Armstrong, OR, USA	American preacher

WHAT MUST I DO TO BE SAVED?

Many have created their own doctrinal followings.

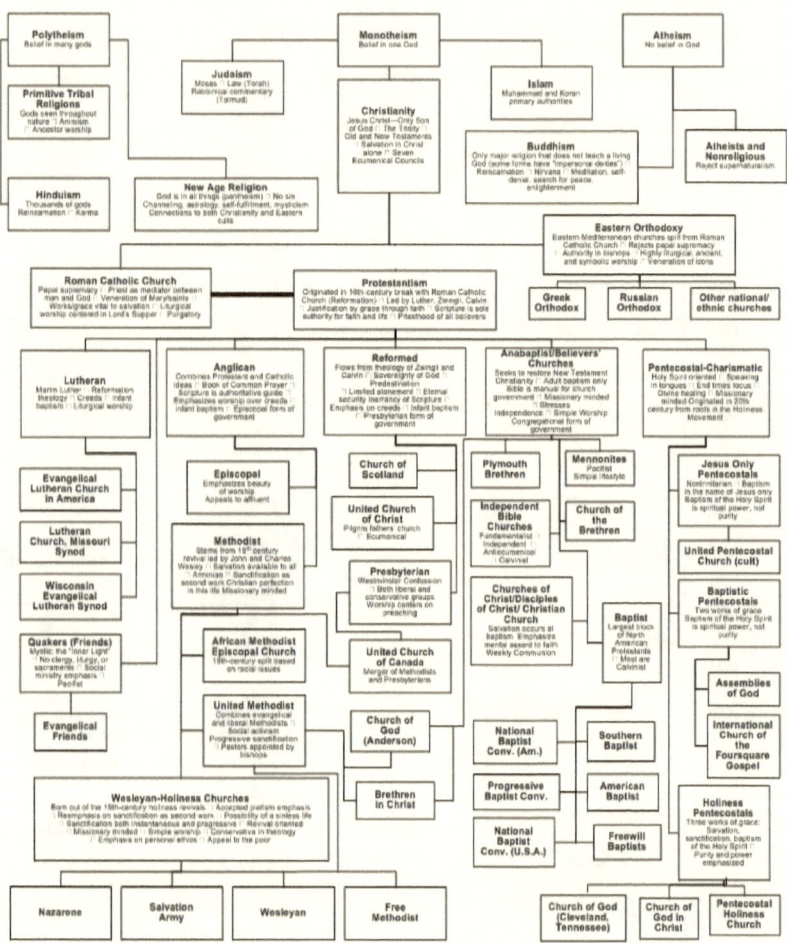

The Narrow Road, the Prophetic Warnings, and the Courage to Follow Christ Alone

The words of Jesus still echo through the centuries:

"Enter through the narrow gate. For wide is the gate and broad is the road that leads to destruction, and many enter through it. But small is the gate and narrow the road that leads to life—and only a few find it."
—Matthew 7:13–14

These are not words of exclusion, but of urgent warning. Jesus was not predicting a statistical minority who happen to find heaven by accident—he was alerting us to the truth that many will claim to know him, but few will actually follow his instructions.

And so it is today. The broad road has become crowded not only with irreligion, but with religious systems, denominations, and personalities that bear the name of Christ but deny the power of the cross—choosing, instead, to follow clever interpretations, human traditions, or culturally fashionable teachings that distract from Jesus' core call: "Follow me."

Paul foresaw this as well. Writing to the early churches, he warned that as soon as the gospel is preached, distortions are sure to follow:

"The time will come when people will not endure sound doctrine, but having itching ears, they will accumulate for themselves teachers to suit their own desires, and will turn away from the truth and wander into myths."
—2 Timothy 4:3–4

In other words, people will begin to follow religion that mirrors their preferences, not the words of Jesus. And they will still feel "spiritual"—they will even appear to be pursuing godliness. But as Paul wrote elsewhere:

"They will have a form of godliness but deny its power."
—2 Timothy 3:5

Let No One Boast in Men

Paul's words to the Corinthians must be heard afresh today, in a world where the cult of personality has saturated not just politics and entertainment, but the church itself. We have made heroes out of pastors, celebrities out of teachers, and denominations out of disagreements. But Paul, with clarity and force, dismantles such thinking:

"Let no one boast in men. For all things are yours—whether Paul or Apollos or Cephas... all are yours, and you are Christ's, and Christ is God's."
—1 Corinthians 3:21-23

In other words, no human leader can claim your allegiance. No denomination can claim ownership over the gospel. You belong to Christ—and to Christ alone.

This is the true freedom of the Christian. Not to discard the church or the body of believers, but to refuse all loyalties that place human teaching above the instruction of Jesus. When any tradition—no matter how noble—obscures the clear message of the gospel, we must have the courage to say: This far, and no further.

Gross Deviations, Brutal Truths, and the Call to Courage

As we continue through this journey, we will inevitably encounter serious departures from the teaching of Jesus, even among well-meaning Christians and communities. Some of these deviations are subtle; others are glaring. But all must be confronted with the same posture: truth in love, courage in humility.

And make no mistake: confronting these things will often reveal brutal truths not just about systems, but about ourselves.

Many will find it far easier to condemn others and excuse themselves, to deconstruct the flaws of other denominations while justifying their own. But if we are to walk the narrow road, we must be willing to examine our own hearts and traditions first, no matter how uncomfortable it makes us.

"Judgment begins with the household of God." —**1 Peter 4:17**

We must remember: our allegiance is not to a denomination, a tradition, or even to our comfort. It is to the risen Christ.

Because on the day when the reality of heaven is revealed, the myths we once cherished—about our superiority, our traditions, or our denominational pride—will be shown for what they are: dust.

The Final Question

And so the question remains—not just for the church at large, but for you:

Will you have the courage to follow Jesus alone?

To lay aside the distractions?

To refuse to boast in men?

To obey his instruction, even when it costs you everything you once clung to?

The wide road is easy, familiar, and well-worn. But it does not lead to life.

"If you continue in my word, then you are truly my disciples."
—John 8:31

False Doctrines

"What Must I Do to Be Saved?" – One Question. One True Answer.

There is no more important question in all of human history than this:

"What must I do to be saved?"

It was asked by trembling jailers, perplexed rulers, earnest crowds, and searching seekers throughout the early church. It echoes through the pages of the New Testament, through every sermon of the apostles, and down the long corridors of Christian history. And yet—astonishingly, heartbreakingly—this question has received many false answers.

But why?

Because, as the apostle Paul warned, many no longer endure sound teaching.

Because, as Jesus foresaw, the road is broad, and many prefer it.

Because there have always been some who, desiring to be teachers of the law, handle the Scriptures without understanding what they are saying or the consequences of what they assert (1 Timothy 1:7).

The truth is, there is only one answer—and it has not changed since the day Peter stood at Pentecost or Paul testified before kings. But false answers have multiplied because:

- Some twist the Scriptures to say what they were never meant to say.
- Some have given themselves over to myths, vain talk, and genealogies that only stir controversy and distract from Christ (1 Timothy 1:3–4).
- Some have surrendered their conscience, trading truth for the comfort of social approval or denominational identity.
- Some, with itching ears, only listen to what they want to hear, rejecting the kind of truth that calls them to change (2 Timothy 4:3).
- And many simply refuse to abandon hypocrisy, preferring a religious identity that costs them nothing but gives the appearance of godliness.

These are not modern problems—they are ancient distortions. But today, more than ever, we must return to the Scriptures and the first-century practices of those who heard the gospel, believed it, and obeyed the instructions of Jesus.

It is not about denomination. It is not about inherited tradition. It is not about feelings or popularity. It is about the unchanging truth of the gospel of the kingdom.

And so now, we turn to that question—not with our own opinions, but with open Bibles and open hearts:

What must I do to be saved?

And we will let God's Word speak.

WHAT MUST I DO TO BE SAVED?

7

What must I do to be saved, Lord?

It becomes increasingly clear, when we attend carefully to the witness of Scripture, that in the formative years following Pentecost, the ekklesia—the gathered community of those who had responded in faithful obedience to Jesus' final commission—was not merely a waiting room for heaven but was, in truth, the kingdom of God breaking forth on earth. This is not to be confused with brick-and-mortar edifices; rather, the kingdom took root in the embodied lives of men and women who had encountered the risen Jesus—either directly or through the faithful testimony of his followers—and responded with believing loyalty.

Conversions in those early days did not hinge upon ornate liturgies or sanctified buildings, but upon the Spirit-filled proclamation of the gospel—the Kerygma—shared across kitchen tables, echoing through prison walls, whispered along dusty roads, and spoken boldly in public squares. This happened precisely because the early Christians had been catechized deeply in the message of Jesus: the message that Israel's long-awaited hope had been fulfilled in him, that through his death and resurrection, sin had been defeated, and that the world was now being summoned to a new allegiance.

What follows, then, is a distillation of that very proclamation—the good news which the early witnesses of Jesus, filled with the Spirit, carried with boldness to every corner of their world.

The Kerygma of the Early Church

At the heart of the early Christian movement was not a set of abstract doctrines or private mystical experiences, but a bold and public proclamation—what the apostles called the kerygma. This was the living tradition, carried first by word of mouth, that bore witness to what God had accomplished in and through Jesus of Nazareth. The apostle Peter, in particular, stands as a central voice in the articulation of this message, a message deeply rooted in Israel's Scriptures and fulfilled in the life, death, and resurrection of the Messiah.

This was not simply a new philosophy. It was the announcement that the story of Israel had reached its long-awaited climax and turning point: the promises made by God throughout the Old Testament were now being fulfilled in Jesus the Christ. The shape of this announcement, repeated with minor variations across the pages of the New Testament, may be summarized as follows:

1. **Jesus was anointed by God at his baptism as the Messiah**, marking him as the one chosen to inaugurate God's kingdom (Acts 10:37).

2. **He began his ministry in Galilee**, calling Israel to repentance and embodying the kingdom in word and deed (Acts 10:38).

3. **His ministry was marked by goodness and power**, healing the sick, casting out demons, and restoring broken lives—acts that bore witness to the inbreaking of God's reign (Mark 10:45; Acts 2:22; 10:38).

4. **Jesus was crucified—according to the determined purpose and foreknowledge of God**, not as a tragic accident but as the decisive moment in God's redemptive plan (Mark 10:45; John 3:16; Acts 2:23; 3:13–15, 18; 4:11; 10:39; 26:23; Rom. 8:34; 1 Cor. 1:17–18; 15:3; Gal. 1:4; Heb. 1:3; 1 Peter 1:2, 19; 3:18; 1 John 4:10).

5. **God raised Jesus from the dead**, vindicating him as Messiah and Lord, and he appeared to his disciples, commissioning them as witnesses of the resurrection (Acts 2:24, 31–32; 3:15, 26; 10:40–41; 17:31; 26:23; Rom. 8:34; 10:9; 1 Cor. 15:4–7, 12ff.; 1 Thess. 1:10; 1 Tim. 3:16; 1 Peter 1:2, 21; 3:18, 21).

6. **Jesus was exalted by God**, enthroned as Lord at God's right hand, sharing in the divine authority and glory (Acts 2:25–29, 33–36; 3:13; 10:36; Rom. 8:34; 10:9; 1 Tim. 3:16; Heb. 1:3; 1 Peter 3:22).

7. **He poured out the Holy Spirit**, forming a new covenant people—Jew and Gentile alike—into a Spirit-filled community bearing witness to the risen King (Acts 1:8; 2:14–18, 33, 38–39; 10:44–47; 1 Peter 1:12).

8. **He will come again**, not to abandon creation but to judge the world in righteousness and to restore all things, bringing God's purposes to their glorious completion (Acts 3:20–21; 10:42; 17:31; 1 Cor. 15:20–28; 1 Thess. 1:10).

9. **All who hear this message are summoned to respond**—to repent, believe, and be baptized—entering the life of God's new creation here and now (Acts 2:21, 38; 3:19; 10:43, 47–48; 17:30; 26:20; Rom. 1:17; 10:9; 1 Peter 3:21).

This proclamation, this apostolic announcement, formed the beating heart of the early Christian mission. Though the various New Testament authors may emphasize different dimensions of it depending on their context and audience, the core remains. Interestingly, the Gospel of Mark—likely reflecting the voice and memory of Peter himself—follows this structure with remarkable clarity, presenting Jesus as the suffering servant who fulfills God's plan through his faithfulness unto death and beyond.

And so, as the early church did, we are confronted not merely with information but with a decision. The Kerygma demands response. It is not passive news but a summons—a call to allegiance, to repentance, and to life under the lordship of the risen Christ. The question remains: how will we answer?

God's Expectation

OBEDIENCE BY FAITH TO THE INSTRUCTION

Hear and Listen to the Message → Believe the Message → Repentance in obedience to the Message → Profess/ Confess Jesus as Lord in Baptism, in obedience to the Message → Saved by faith demonstrated in obedience, as long as you do not fall away from God to old life of sin

Do not believe the Message → Rejects God's appeal to you. No salvation till you accept the message, repent and obey, by faith in baptism

Holy Spirit gives you strength and helps you to trust and obey the teachings in scriptures. More obedient older Christians teach you, by example, to obey Jesus' teachings.

Before anyone can fully grasp the significance of salvation offered through Jesus the Messiah, they must reckon with a series of key decision points—moments of clarity where the heart is summoned to respond. These are not merely intellectual checkpoints, but spiritual invitations to realignment, to transformation, to covenant.

The prophet Isaiah declares, with poetic precision and prophetic urgency:

"As the rain and the snow come down from heaven, and do not return to it without watering the earth and making it bud and flourish, so that it yields seed for the sower and bread for the eater, so is my word that goes out from my mouth:
It will not return to me empty, but will accomplish what I desire and achieve the purpose for which I sent it" (Isaiah 55:10–11).

Here, Isaiah is not speaking in metaphor alone. He is articulating the deep conviction that the word of God—whether it comes through law, prophecy, gospel, or Spirit-inspired teaching—has a telos, a goal. It is not static. It is sent, like the rain, to do something. And what it does, first and foremost, is to uncover, to illumine, and to transform. It reveals not only the heart of God, but also the hidden places of our own hearts. And perhaps most poignantly, it shows what happens when we resist it.

Thus, the first decision point for anyone standing at the threshold of faith in Christ is this:

Will we receive the Scriptures as God's authoritative word—trustworthy and true, living and active, the standard by which all questions of faith, identity, and purpose must be measured?

This is no small matter. In a world swirling with competing truths and half-formed ideologies, the authority of the Bible is not merely about religious correctness. It is about whether we will allow God's revealed word to shape us—to interpret us—rather than insisting on interpreting it according to our own preferences or suspicions. The early Christians did not inherit a set of abstract doctrines; they received the Scriptures as the story of God's covenant faithfulness, now fulfilled in Jesus. To embrace that story is to step into it, to let it narrate us into God's purposes.

If we cannot begin here, then every other step in the journey of salvation is rendered uncertain. But if we do, the rain begins to fall, the seed begins to sprout—and the Word begins to do its work.

The written word of God

To truly grasp the place the Bible must hold in the life of anyone seeking to respond to God's saving invitation, we must turn to the wise and deeply pastoral words of the apostle Paul to a young man he had mentored in the faith. In a moment of sobering clarity, Paul writes:

"But as for you, continue in what you have learned and have become convinced of, because you know those from whom you learned it, and how from infancy you have known the Holy Scriptures, which are able to make you wise for salvation through faith in Christ Jesus. All Scripture is God-breathed and is useful for teaching, rebuking, correcting and training in righteousness, so that the man of God may be thoroughly equipped for every good work."
(2 Timothy 3:14-16)

Paul begins this passage, not in abstraction, but in the very concrete reality of a world where spiritual confusion and moral chaos abound. He had already warned Timothy of a time when many would maintain a veneer of godliness—external religion—while their lives were altogether detached from the transforming power of God. Into this climate of instability, Paul speaks with conviction: "continue in what you have learned." Why? Because what Timothy had received from childhood, through faithful instruction, was not merely human wisdom—it was the sacred writings.

At the time Paul penned these words, "the Scriptures" referred primarily to the Law and the Prophets—the Torah and the Writings—which Timothy, a Jewish believer, would have known from his earliest days. These were not just cultural artifacts or devotional texts; they were, and are, the very breath of God—God's own speech mediated through human words. They bear divine authority, and they carry within them the power to make one "wise for salvation through faith in Christ Jesus."

What Paul makes clear—both to Timothy and to us—is that the Scriptures are God's primary means of shaping and equipping His people. They do not simply inform; they form. They train the people of God to recognize what is true, to reject what is false, to walk the path of righteousness, and to be equipped for the works of love and justice that characterize God's kingdom.

So then, this leads us again to the first great decision point in the journey toward embracing salvation in Jesus:

Will we accept the Bible—Old and New Testament alike—as God's inspired, authoritative word, and as the final standard for matters of faith, truth, and how life ought to be lived?

The Scriptures are not incidental to faith; they are instrumental. To claim faith in Christ while dismissing the authority of the Word that reveals him is to sever the root from the tree. The Bible is not simply a book of helpful sayings or ancient wisdom; it is the divinely-inspired witness of God's dealings with His world, culminating in Christ, and it speaks today with the same force: to teach, to correct, to train, and to transform.

The Old Testament Books (The Scriptures Jesus had)

	JEWISH BIBLE	ORTHODOX BIBLE	ETHIOPIAN BIBLE	CATHOLIC BIBLE	PROTESTANT BIBLE
TORAH - The Five Books of Moses	1 Genesis 2 Exodus 3 Leviticus 4 Numbers 5 Deuteronomy	1 Genesis 2 Exodus 3 Leviticus 4 Numbers 5 Deuteronomy	1 Genesis 2 Exodus 3 Leviticus 4 Numbers 5 Deuteronomy	1 Genesis 2 Exodus 3 Leviticus 4 Numbers 5 Deuteronomy	1 Genesis 2 Exodus 3 Leviticus 4 Numbers 5 Deuteronomy
NEVI'IM - The Eight Books of the Prophets	6 Joshua 7 Judges 8 1 Samuel 9 2 Samuel 10 1 Kings 11 2 Kings 12 Isaiah 13 Jeremiah 14 Ezekiel	6 Joshua 7 Judges 8 Ruth 9 1 Kingdoms (1 Samuel) 10 2 Kingdoms (2 Samuel) 11 3 Kingdoms (1 Kings) 12 4 Kingdoms (2 Kings) 13 1 Chronicles 14 2 Chronicles	6 Enoch 7 Jubilees 8 Joshua 9 Judges 10 Ruth 11 1 Samuel 12 2 Samuel 13 1 Kings 14 2 Kings	6 Joshua 7 Judges 8 Ruth 9 1 Kingdoms (1 Samuel) 10 2 Kingdoms (2 Samuel) 11 3 Kingdoms (1 Kings) 12 4 Kingdoms (2 Kings) 13 1 Chronicles 14 2 Chronicles	6 Joshua 7 Judges 8 Ruth 9 1 Samuel 10 2 Samuel 11 1 Kings 12 2 Kings 13 1 Chronicles 14 2 Chronicles
NEVI'IM - The Twelve Minor Prophets	15 Hosea 16 Joel 17 Amos 18 Obadiah 19 Jonah 20 Micah 21 Nahum 22 Habakkuk 23 Zephaniah 24 Haggai 25 Zechariah 26 Malachi	15 Ezra 16 2 Ezra 17 Nehemiah 18 Tobit 19 Judith 20 Esther 21 1 Maccabees 22 2 Maccabees 23 3 Maccabees 24 Psalms (151 in number) 25 Job 26 Proverbs of Solomon	15 1 Chronicles 16 2 Chronicles 17 Ezra 18 Nehemiah 19 3rd Ezra 20 4th Ezra 21 Tobit 22 Judith 23 Esther 24 1 Macabees 25 2 Macabees 26 3 Macabees	15 1 Esdras 16 2 Esdras (Nehemiah) 17 Tobit 18 Judith 19 Esther 20 1 Maccabees 21 2 Maccabees 22 3 Maccabees 23 Psalms (151 in number) 24 Job 25 Proverbs of Solomon 26 Ecclesiastes	15 Ezra 16 Nehemiah 17 Esther 18 Job 19 Psalms 20 Proverbs 21 Ecclesiastes 22 8.Song of Solomon 23 Isaiah 24 Jeremiah 25 Lamentations 26 Ezekiel
KETHUVIM - The Eleven Books of the Writings	27 Psalms 28 Proverbs 29 Job 30 Song of Songs 31 Ruth 32 Lamentations 33 Ecclesiastes 34 Esther 35 Daniel 36 Ezra 37 Nehemiah 38 1 Chronicles 39 2 Chronicles	27 Ecclesiastes 28 Song of Songs 29 Wisdom of Solomon 30 Wisdom of Sirach 31 Hosea 32 Amos 33 Micah 34 Joel 35 Obadiah 36 Jonah 37 Nahum 38 Habakkuk 39 Zephaniah 40 Haggai 41 Zechariah 42 Malachi 43 Isaiah 44 Jeremiah 45 Baruch 46 Lamentation of Jeremiah 47 Epistle of Jeremiah 48 Ezekiel 49 Daniel	27 Job 28 Psalms 29 Proverbs 30 Taagsas (Proverbs 25-31) 31 Wisdom of Solomon 32 Ecclesiastes 33 Song of Solomon 34 Sirach (Ecclesiasticus) 35 Isaiah 36 Jeremiah 37 Baruch 38 Lamentations 39 Ezekiel 40 Daniel 41 Hosea 42 Amos 43 Micah 44 Joel 45 Obadiah 46 Jonah 47 Nahum 48 Habakkuk 49 Zephaniah 50 Haggai 51 Zechariah 52 Malachi	27 Song of Songs 28 Wisdom of Solomon 29 Sirach (Ecclesiasticus) 30 Hosea 31 Amos 32 Micah 33 Joel 34 Obadiah 35 Jonah 36 Nahum 37 Habakkuk 38 Zephaniah 39 Haggai 40 Zechariah 41 Malachi 42 Isaiah 43 Jeremiah 44 Baruch 45 Lamentation of Jeremiah 46 Ezekiel 47 Daniel	27 Daniel 28 Hosea 29 Joel 30 Amos 31 Obadiah 32 Jonah 33 Micah 34 Nahum 35 Habakkuk 36 Zephaniah 37 Haggai 38 Zechariah 39 Malachi

Paul reminds Timothy with a deeply personal and pastoral tone: "Ever since you were a child, you have known the Holy Scriptures"—not merely as texts to be memorized, but as the living story in which his own life had been immersed. These sacred writings, Paul insists, are not static relics of the past, but are able to make you wise for salvation through faith in Christ Jesus (2 Timothy 3:15). That is, they carry within them a divine logic, a Spirit-formed wisdom that leads the faithful toward the fullness of God's saving purposes.

What is especially striking here is Paul's unequivocal conviction that Scripture is sufficient—not in the sense of limiting God, but in recognizing that the Bible is the God-given means by which a believer is shaped, matured, and made ready for every good work (2 Timothy 3:17). It is not one resource among many. It is the resource, the foundational instrument through which God speaks, corrects, trains, and equips those who seek to live in faithful obedience.

The Scriptures are not simply a guidebook for private piety or moral instruction; they are the narrative in which we learn what God has done, is doing, and will do for His world through Jesus the Messiah. They form the covenant framework in which believers discover who God is, who they are, and how they are to live as part of God's new creation.

So we return once again to that crucial decision point:

Will we take the Scriptures—the Bible—as God's authoritative, inspired word, capable not only of revealing truth but of reshaping our entire way of life in light of Christ?

If we will, then like rain on parched soil, the Word will begin to bear fruit. It will not return empty. It will fulfill the purpose for which God has sent it.

WHAT MUST I DO TO BE SAVED?

Books of the New Testament and purpose.

BOOK	AUTHOR	TIME OF WRITING[1]	PLACE OF WRITING	ADDRESSEES
Galatians	Paul	49, just after 1st missionary journey	Antioch in Syria (?)	Christians in Pisidian Antioch, Iconium, Lystra, Derbe, and southern Galatia
1 Thessalonians	Paul	50-51, during 2nd missionary journey	Corinth	Christians in Thessalonica
2 Thessalonians	Paul	50-51, during 2nd missionary journey	Corinth	Christians in Thessalonica
1 Corinthians	Paul	54, during 3rd missionary journey	Ephesus	Christians in Corinth
2 Corinthians	Paul	55, during 3rd missionary journey	Macedonia	Christians in Corinth
Romans	Paul	55 during 3rd missionary journey	Corinth	Christians in Rome
James	James, half brother of Jesus	40s or 50s	Probably Jerusalem	Jewish Christians of the Dispersion
Mark	John Mark	Late 50s or early 60s	Rome	Non-Christian Romans; new converts
Philemon	Paul	60	Rome	Philemon, his family, and the church in his house at Colosse
Colossians	Paul	60	Rome	Christians in Colosse
Ephesians	Paul	60	Rome	Christians in the region around Ephesus
Luke	Luke	60	Probably Caesarea or Rome	Non-Christian Roman official, possibly other cultured non-Christians
Acts	Luke	61	Rome	Same as above
Philippians	Paul	61	Rome	Christians in Philippi
1 Timothy	Paul	62	Macedonia	Timothy in Ephesus
Titus	Paul	62	Nicopolis	Titus in Crete
2 Timothy	Paul	63	Rome	Timothy in Ephesus
1 Peter	Peter	63	Rome	Christians in Asia Minor
2 Peter	Peter	63-64	Rome	Christians in Asia Minor
Matthew	Matthew	60s	Probably Antioch in Syria	Jews in Syria or Palestine
Hebrews	Unknown[2] (Apollos, Luke, Barnabas, Priscilla?)	60s	Unknown	Jewish Christians in Rome or Jerusalem
Jude	Jude, half brother of Jesus	60s or 70s	Unknown	Christians in general
John	John	Late 80s or early 90s	Ephesus	Christians and/or non-Christians in the region around Ephesus
1 John	John	Late 80s or early 90s	Ephesus	Christians in the region around Ephesus
2 John	John	Late 80s or early 90s	Ephesus	A church near Ephesus
3 John	John	Late 80s or early 90s	Ephesus	Gaius, a Christians in the region around Ephesus
Revelation	John	Late 80s or early 90s	Patmos, off coast of Asia Minor	Seven churches in western Asia Minor

It is essential to recognize that when Jesus speaks of "the Scriptures," he is referring to what we now call the Old Testament—more specifically, to the Law and the Prophets, the sacred writings of the Hebrew Bible. Time and again, Jesus frames his mission and identity in relation to these texts. He tells his followers, "Do not think that I have come to abolish the Law or the Prophets; I have not come to abolish them but to fulfill them" (Matthew 5:17). The Scriptures, in Jesus' view, are not background noise—they are the stage upon which the drama of God's redemptive plan is playing out, with him at the very center.

Yet over time, the church's relationship with the Bible has become complicated, shaped by historical events such as the Reformation. The split led by figures like Martin Luther and John Calvin from the Roman Catholic Church gave rise to what we now call the Protestant tradition and its distinctive version of the biblical canon, largely adopted by Western denominational churches. Meanwhile, the Eastern churches—emerging from the earlier schism with Rome—have preserved a different biblical tradition, one that has, remarkably, avoided the same level of fragmentation seen in the West.

Among the oldest and most expansive collections of biblical texts is found in the Ethiopian Orthodox Church, whose canon includes books long revered in the early Christian centuries. Such diversity in canon reminds us that the formation of the Bible, though guided by the Spirit, occurred through real historical processes and within real communities.

And yet, despite this rich heritage, we find ourselves in an age where Scripture is often neglected—even by those who claim to belong to Christ. The failure is not primarily intellectual, but spiritual: a failure of trust. People may profess faith, but many live guided by other authorities:

- Some follow what simply feels right in their own eyes.
- Others embrace a selective faith, picking and choosing verses to suit personal preferences.
- Still others dismiss the Scriptures altogether, claiming that they are no longer relevant in the modern world.

But the word of God is anything but outdated. It is alive. As the writer to the Hebrews puts it:

"For the word of God is living and active. Sharper than any double-edged sword, it penetrates even to dividing soul and spirit, joints and marrow; it judges the thoughts and attitudes of the heart. Nothing in all creation is hidden from God's sight. Everything is uncovered and laid bare before the eyes of him to whom we must give account."
(Hebrews 4:12–14)

This is not the description of an ancient relic, but of a present-tense force—God's very voice, still speaking, still piercing, still transforming. The Scriptures hold up a mirror to the human heart, revealing not just our failures but our deep need for grace, and the shape of the life we are called to live in the Messiah.

Thus, we are brought back again to that foundational decision:

Will we allow the Bible, in its God-breathed authority, to serve not merely as a reference point, but as the compass for our lives?

Until we settle that question, every other decision in the journey of faith will remain unstable. But if we will trust the Word, we will find it is not dead ink on a page—it is breath, it is light, it is life.

The writer of Hebrews offers not only a vision of the living, active Word of God—but also a sobering warning. Just as the ancient people of Israel fell into judgment for failing to heed what God had spoken in the past, so too does the danger remain for us. The verse preceding that well-known declaration about the power of Scripture reminds us of this:

"So I declared on oath in my anger, 'They shall never enter my rest.'" (Hebrews 4:11)

This is not mere historical observation. It is a prophetic caution: when God speaks, history moves—and those who disregard His word find themselves at odds with the very story they are meant to inhabit.

Indeed, the word of God remains alive precisely because the human condition has not changed. Yes, the circumstances of modern life have shifted—our technologies, our systems, even our languages—but the human heart remains subject to the same pride, the same rebellion, the same longing for self-rule that plagued ancient Israel. What Scripture reveals about the human soul is as true now as it was then.

And yet, despite this truth, there remain three powerful barriers that often prevent people—even professing Christians—from submitting to Scripture as the standard for life, values, and faith:

1. A reliance on what "feels" right or seems right in one's own eyes

– This is the ancient temptation of Eden: to define good and evil on our own terms. It is seductive, but it always leads to distortion.

2. A selective approach to belief—picking and choosing

– Like a buffet, many approach the Bible taking what is convenient and leaving what is challenging. But Scripture is not ours to edit; it is ours to receive.

3. The modern dismissal that the Bible is "outdated"

– Many assume that ancient words cannot address contemporary complexities. But as Hebrews 4 reminds us, the Word of God transcends time—it pierces the heart precisely because it speaks to what is unchanging in us.

Paul warned the early church in Corinth against this very drift. He wrote:

"Do not go beyond what is written." ~ 1 Corinthians 4:6

That is the line—the guardrail—that keeps us anchored in apostolic faith. The temptation to innovate, to substitute the wisdom of our age for the truth handed down, is as strong now as it was then. And yet, the path of faithfulness has always been the path of fidelity to the Scriptures—God's written word, the apostolic witness, the testimony of those who saw and heard and walked with the risen Lord.

This, then, forms the continued challenge of the first decision point:

Will we allow the whole of Scripture—not just the parts we prefer—to shape our worldview, our conduct, our identity, and our hope? Or will we go beyond what is written, and thus drift from the truth entrusted to the saints?

The Word of God is not just true; it is formative. It does not merely inform—it transforms, if we will only let it.

One of the most subtle, yet serious, ways we drift from the authority of Scripture is through the lens of private interpretation—a deeply modern and individualized way of approaching the text that detaches it from the community of faith, the apostolic witness, and the guiding presence of the Holy Spirit. The result is not freedom, but fragmentation.

The apostle Peter, reflecting with great sobriety on the nature of the prophetic word, writes:

"And we have the word of the prophets made more certain, and you will do well to pay attention to it, as to a light shining in a dark place, until the day dawns and the morning star rises in your hearts. Above all, you must understand that no prophecy of Scripture came about by the prophet's own interpretation.
For prophecy never had its origin in the will of man, but men spoke from God as they were carried along by the Holy Spirit."
(2 Peter 1:19-21)

Here Peter affirms that Scripture is not a collection of religious musings or private reflections. It is God-breathed, brought into being through the work of the Holy Spirit. The prophets did not write simply what they felt; they wrote what they were moved to write—carried along by a divine impulse that rooted their words in God's purposes. And for that reason, Peter urges the church to pay attention—like travelers in the night looking to a lamp to guide their steps until daybreak.

To remove Scripture from its context—whether by imposing modern ideologies onto it, reading it in isolation from its story, or reducing it to a tool for personal affirmation—is to distort its power and intention. Private interpretation, when divorced from the apostolic faith and the Spirit-filled community of the church, becomes a vehicle not for revelation but for confusion.

This is why the early church rooted its reading of Scripture in the person and work of Jesus, the risen Lord, and interpreted the Law and the Prophets in light of his death and resurrection. It is also why they read and lived the Scriptures together—not as individuals shaping truth to their preferences, but as a body being shaped by the truth.

So we must ask again:

Will we submit to the Word of God as it was given—through the Spirit, within the community, pointing always to Christ—or will we insist on making it serve our private meanings, our personal narratives, our isolated perspectives?

The light is still shining. The prophetic word is still certain. But we will only walk in that light if we resist the temptation to privatize it—and instead let the Spirit who inspired it be the one who interprets and applies it through the body of Christ.

WHAT MUST I DO TO BE SAVED?

The New Testament Books (Writings by Jesus' disciples after his death and resurrection)

#	NEW TESTAMENT BOOKS	ORTHODOX	ETHIOPIAN BIBLE	CATHOLIC BIBLE	PROTESTANT BIBLE
1	The Gospel of Mark	Mark	1 Mark	1 Mark	1 Mark
2	The Gospel of Matthew	Matthew	2 Matthew	2 Matthew	2 Matthew
3	The Gospel of Luke	Luke	3 Luke	3 Luke	3 Luke
4	The Gospel of John	John	4 John	4 John	4 John
5	First Letter of Paul, Silvanus, and Timothy to the Church of Thessalonica	1 Thessalonians	5 1 Thessalonians	5 1 Thessalonians	5 Acts of the Apostles
6	Second Letter of Paul, Silvanus, and Timothy to the Church of Thessalonica	2 Thessalonians	6 2 Thessalonians	6 2 Thessalonians	6 Romans
7	Letter of Paul and Sosthenes to the Church of the Corinthians Sanctified and Called Saints	1 Corinthians	7 1 Corinthians	7 1 Corinthians	7 1 Corinthians
8	Letter of Paul and Timothy to the Church of the Corinthians	2 Corinthians	8 2 Corinthians	8 2 Corinthians	8 2 Corinthians
9	Letter of Paul and the Brethren with him to the Churches of the Galatians	Galatians	9 Galatians	9 Galatians	9 Galatians
10	Letter of Paul to the Beloved of God Called Saints Dwelling in Rome	Romans	10 Romans	10 Romans	10 Ephesians
11	Letter of Paul to the Faithful Saints Dwelling in Ephesus	Ephesians	11 Ephesians	11 Ephesians	11 Philippians
12	Letter of Paul and Timothy to the Saints accompanying the Bishops and Deacons in Philippi	Philippians	12 Philippians	12 Philippians	12 Colossians
13	Letter of Paul and Timothy to the Saints and Faithful Brethren Dwelling in Colosse (Colossians)	Colossians	13 Colossians	13 Colossians	13 1 Thessalonians
14	Letter of Paul and Timothy to Philemon, Apphia, Archippus, and their House Church	Philemon	14 Philemon	14 Philemon	14 2 Thessalonians
15	Letter of Paul to Titus	Titus	15 Titus	15 Titus	15 1 Timothy
16	First Letter of Paul to Timothy	1 Timothy	16 1 Timothy	16 1 Timothy	16 2 Timothy
17	Second Letter of Paul to Timothy	2 Timothy	17 2 Timothy	17 2 Timothy	17 Titus
18	Letter of James to the Dispersed Twelve Tribes of Israel	James	18 James	18 James	18 Philemon
19	Letter of Jude to those who are Called, Sanctified by God, and Preserved in the Messiah	Jude	19 Jude	19 Jude	19 Hebrews
20	Letter of Peter to the Elect Pilgrims of the Dispersion in Pontus, Galatia, Cappadocia, Asia, and Bithynia	1 Peter	20 1 Peter	20 1 Peter	20 James
21	Letter of Peter to the Receivers of Faith by the Righteousness of the Messiah	2 Peter	21 2 Peter	21 2 Peter	21 1 Peter
22	Letter of John to Those Who Have Ceased From Willful Sins	1 John	22 1 John	22 1 John	22 2 Peter
23	Letter of John to Kuria and Her Children	2 John	23 2 John	23 2 John	23 1 John
24	Letter of John to Gaius	3 John	24 3 John	24 3 John	24 2 John
25	Chronicles of the Apostles	Acts of the Apostles	25 Acts of the Apostles	25 Acts of the Apostles	25 3 John
26	Letter of Barnabas to the Churches of the Hebrews	Hebrews	26 Hebrews	26 Hebrews	26 Jude
27	Revelation - Visions of John	Revelation of John	27 Revelation of John	27 Revelation of John	27 Revelation of John
28	Letter of Barnabas to the Gentiles	Barnabas	28 Shepherd of Hermas		
29	Letter of Paul to the Brethren Dwelling in Laodicea	Laodiceans	29 1 Clement		
30	Letter of the Church in Rome to the Church of Corinth who are Called and Sanctified by the Will of God	1 Clement	30 2 Clement		
31	Letter of Clement to the Church of Corinth	2 Clement			

In his second letter, addressed to Christians living in a world not unlike our own—turbulent, pluralistic, and full of competing voices—the apostle Peter reminds the early church of a crucial truth: God has already given us everything we need for life and godliness. Not through mystical speculation or abstract philosophy, but through his promises, anchored in his Word. These divine promises, Peter writes, are not vague spiritual sentiments; they are the means by which we become participants in the divine nature (2 Peter 1:3–4).

And so, Peter urges his readers to pay close attention—to hold fast to the Scriptures like a lamp shining in a dark place. But then he issues a clear and urgent warning:

"Above all, you must understand that no prophecy of Scripture came about by the prophet's own interpretation.
For prophecy never had its origin in the will of man, but men spoke from God as they were carried along by the Holy Spirit."
(2 Peter 1:20–21)

This is a watershed moment. Peter wants his readers—and us—to grasp that the Word of God is not open to freeform speculation or private manipulation. The origin of Scripture is divine, not human; the prophets spoke not from impulse, nor invention, but as they were borne along by the Holy Spirit. That means interpretation is not a personal playground. It is a sacred task, undertaken in humility, in community, and under the guidance of the same Spirit who inspired the words in the first place.

If we look to the life of Jesus—the very Word made flesh—we do not find a disjointed, incoherent message. His teaching is not erratic. His conversations are not filled with contradiction. His life is the perfect fulfillment of the Law and the Prophets, and his words echo with the unmistakable harmony of divine truth.

And yet, time after time, those who walked away from Jesus did so because they could not—or would not—receive what he said. They tried to interpret him on their own terms, fit him into their frameworks, or twist his words to meet their expectations. And failing that, they simply turned back.

This is why we must be clear:

There is only one true message God intends through the Scriptures—not a plurality of meanings tailored to every reader's desire, but a singular, Spirit-given truth revealed in Christ and meant to be received through faithful listening.

In an age dominated by relativism, where meaning is often treated as fluid and personal, this may sound countercultural. But it is the very foundation of faith: God has spoken, and His Word is not confused. It is coherent. It is clear. And it is calling us—not to reimagine it, but to be reimagined by it.

B. Traditions or Customs

In a striking confrontation that reverberates through every generation of the church, Jesus exposes a critical failure—not of atheism or rebellion, but of religiosity divorced from God's heart. The scene unfolds in Mark 7, where the Pharisees and scribes, men highly regarded for their piety and rigorous devotion to the law, challenge Jesus over a seemingly minor ritual: the ceremonial washing of hands.

"Why don't your disciples live according to the tradition of the elders," they ask, *"instead of eating their food with unclean hands?"*
(Mark 7:5)

Now, to the modern reader, this might seem like a dispute over hygiene. But this was no debate about cleanliness—it was about righteousness. The Pharisees, in their zeal, had constructed layer upon layer of oral tradition around the Law of Moses. Their logic was clear: if the Law is perfect and divine, then it must speak, either explicitly or implicitly, to every conceivable aspect of life. And so, over time, they expanded God's commands into an intricate web of rules, regulations, and rituals, attempting to legislate holiness into every corner of daily existence.

But in doing so, they lost sight of something essential: the heart of the Law.

Jesus responds not with niceties but with piercing truth:

"Isaiah was right when he prophesied about you hypocrites... These people honor me with their lips, but their hearts are far from me. They worship me in vain; their teachings are but rules taught by men. You have let go of the commands of God and are holding on to the traditions of men."
(Mark 7:6–8)

This is not just a first-century critique. It is a prophetic word to every age where human systems—however well-intended—are allowed to displace the authority of God's Word. The traditions of the elders were not inherently evil, but they became dangerous when they replaced the commands of God, or worse, rendered them void.

What Jesus confronts here is the tragic irony of a deeply religious people who have built fences around the Word of God in the name of reverence, but who end up honoring the fences instead of the Word itself. Their effort to protect the Law had, over time, distorted it—transforming a covenant of grace into a burdensome code of external compliance.

This leads us to another false standard that can subtly draw us away from true Scriptural authority:

The elevation of human tradition—religious, denominational, or cultural—above the plain teaching of Scripture.

When traditions are used to clarify or celebrate truth, they can be beautiful. But when they cause us to ignore or override God's commands, they become idols. And as Jesus makes plain, when worship is built on such foundations, it is in vain. It becomes performance, not communion.

So the decision point is once again before us:

Will we allow Scripture to critique and shape our traditions, or will we cling to traditions so tightly that we nullify the very Word we claim to uphold?

Jesus' warning is clear: not all devotion is true worship. And not every tradition, however cherished, leads us toward the heart of God.

C. Facts or Feelings

There's a pivotal moment in John's Gospel when, having seen his signs and heard his words, many put their faith in him (John 8:30). But Jesus, never content with superficial allegiance, offers a clarifying word—one that cuts through the excitement of the crowd and goes to the very heart of what it means to follow him:

"If you hold to my teaching, you are really my disciples.
Then you will know the truth, and the truth will set you free."
(John 8:31–32)

The distinction Jesus draws here is critical. Belief is the beginning—but holding to his teaching is the mark of genuine discipleship. One can believe in a truth, admire it, even speak of it publicly. But only those who live by it, who allow it to shape their habits, their decisions, their hopes and identities—only these, Jesus says, will come to know the truth that liberates.

To bring it into everyday language, consider the person who believes in the effectiveness of a diet. Belief alone does not lead to transformation. One must commit—live by the plan, adjust one's lifestyle, practice discipline. It is the implementation of belief that produces freedom from what previously held one captive.

So it is with Jesus' teaching. The life of faith is not about mental assent or cultural Christianity—it is about obedient loyalty to the words of the Messiah. Knowing his teaching is not merely about information; it is about immersion—habitually reading, meditating on, and practicing the Scriptures. Only then does the truth begin to do its work, setting us free from sin, fear, and self-deception.

Jesus reinforces this again in Matthew's Gospel:

"Not everyone who says to me, 'Lord, Lord,' will enter the kingdom of heaven, but only the one who does the will of my Father who is in heaven." ~ (Matthew 7:21)

And later, with equal clarity in John's Gospel, Jesus says:

"As for the person who hears my words but does not keep them, I do not judge him. For I did not come to judge the world, but to save it. There is a judge for the one who rejects me and does not accept my words; that very word which I spoke will condemn him at the last day."
(John 12:47-48)

This is not the voice of a tyrant. This is the voice of truth incarnate, lovingly warning those he longs to save. His words are not merely good advice. They are the standard by which all humanity will one day be measured. To reject his words is not to sidestep a personal preference—it is to reject the very fabric of the new creation he is ushering in.

So the next decision point is this:

Will we not only believe in Jesus, but live by his words—holding fast to his teaching as our daily guide, our rule of life, and our source of true freedom?

The Word has been spoken. It has been made flesh. It is living and active. And it will either liberate us now—or confront us at the end. The choice is ours.

The First Decision point

The First Decision Point: Submitting to the Scriptures as the Standard

In a world full of spiritual noise—many claiming to follow Jesus, many bearing the label "Christian"—Jesus himself provides a clear and uncompromising measure of true discipleship. It is not rooted in identity, affiliation, or sentiment, but in obedient faithfulness to his teaching.

"If you hold to my teaching, you are really my disciples. Then you will know the truth, and the truth will set you free." ~ (John 8:31–32)

Notice carefully: not everyone who believes is called a disciple. The ones Jesus affirms are those who remain in his word—who adopt his teaching not as occasional inspiration, but as the framework of their lives. They hear, trust, and practice what he says. And it is in this obedience that true freedom—freedom from sin, guilt, fear, and falsehood—is found.

According to Jesus, then, a faithful, obedient disciple is a saved person. Conversely, the person who believes but does not live by his teaching remains outside of that saving relationship. This is not harshness. It is clarity—truth spoken in love, that we might truly live.

And so we arrive at the first and foundational decision in answering that most urgent of questions: "What must I do to be saved?"

We must begin here:

Will we receive the Bible—the Scriptures—as the final, God-given standard for all matters of faith, obedience, and salvation?

Not theological systems. Not denominational traditions. Not extra-biblical writings, however thoughtful.

It is in the Scriptures that we meet the real Jesus. It is in the Gospels, the Prophets, the Letters, the Psalms, that the message of the kingdom is proclaimed and the forgiveness of sins is announced. To go elsewhere first is to bypass the one voice that truly matters.

Only when we allow the Bible to speak—unfiltered, unmuted, unmanipulated—do we come face to face with the Christ who saves. And only then can we take our first step as true disciples: to hear his words, trust them, obey them, and be set free.

Final Instruction on Salvation: The Great Commission as the Heart of the Gospel Mission

As the risen Jesus stood before his disciples on a Galilean mountain, his final words were not a farewell but a commissioning—a declaration of authority and a mandate that would define the movement we now call the Church. This was not a private word for a few elite followers. It was a public summons, spoken with cosmic authority and global intention:

"All authority in heaven and on earth has been given to me. Therefore go and make disciples of all nations, baptizing them in the name of the Father and of the Son and of the Holy Spirit, and teaching them to obey everything I have commanded you. And surely I am with you always, to the very end of the age."
(Matthew 28:18-20)

This is not merely a mission statement. It is the will of Jesus Christ—the resurrected Lord, the true King of the world. It is his blueprint for salvation, extended to every person, in every nation, across every generation. Whether black or white, Asian or Arab, rich or poor, skeptic or seeker, the invitation is the same: come, become a disciple.

And what does that entail?

1. To become a disciple—not simply a believer in abstract truths, but one who follows Jesus in loyal obedience, learning his way of life as the path to true freedom.

2. To be baptized—not as a symbolic gesture only, but as an embodied act of dying to the old self and rising into the life of the kingdom. Baptism is the public and spiritual initiation into the new creation life Jesus inaugurates.

3. To be taught to obey—for discipleship is not about information but transformation. Jesus does not ask merely to be admired; he commands us to live by his teaching—by grace, in community, and through the power of the Spirit.

This is the shape of salvation. It is not a one-time prayer or an abstract belief. It is a life reoriented around Jesus—his teaching, his community, his mission. It begins with the authority of Christ, moves outward through the obedience of faith, and continues until the whole world has heard and responded.

So then, if we truly ask, "What must I do to be saved?"—we must hear Jesus' answer in full:

Become a disciple. Be baptized. Be taught to obey. And follow him—every day, in every way, until the end.

This is not a burdensome command. It is an invitation to walk with the risen King, who has promised to be with us, not only at the beginning, but "to the very end of the age."

The Second Decision point

A Call to Examine: Are You Truly a Disciple of Jesus?

Let us now come to the most personal—and perhaps the most important—question of all:

Are you a disciple of Jesus?

Not simply, "Do you believe in God?"

Not even, "Do you go to church?"

But rather: Have you responded to Jesus in the way he instructed?

"Examine yourselves to see whether you are in the faith; test yourselves. Do you not realize that Christ Jesus is in you—unless, of course, you fail the test?"
(2 Corinthians 13:5)

Paul's challenge to the Corinthian believers is not meant to induce anxiety, but clarity. He is not encouraging doubt for its own sake, but inviting every person to take stock of their life in light of the message of Christ. Have we responded to Jesus on his terms, or our own?

So consider this:

- When did you become a disciple?

- How did you become saved—what did that journey look like?

- Who taught you the message of Jesus—not merely about him, but what he commanded?

- Were you baptized in response to that message, as Jesus instructed in Matthew 28:18–20?

These are not technicalities. These are the markers of obedience that Jesus himself established as the path into life with him. And to avoid these questions—or to answer them vaguely—is to risk assuming a spiritual identity that has no foundation in the gospel.

It is worth drawing a timeline of your life: tracing your spiritual journey from childhood to now, laying it honestly alongside the teachings of Jesus and the practices of the early church. What do you find?

The truth is, many people today have inherited a form of religion that lacks the substance of discipleship. Some were raised in Christian households but never taught what Jesus actually requires. Others have wandered from church to church, absorbing traditions and impressions but never encountering the full message of salvation. And tragically, many churches today have become places of attendance rather than places of transformation, where few are asked the hard but holy question: Are you actually following Jesus as he instructed?

In the New Testament, no one became a Christian by simply attending a worship service. People came to faith because they met disciples—men and women who had been taught the message, who believed, who obeyed, and who could clearly pass that message on. They heard the gospel, believed it, repented, and were baptized in the name of Jesus for the forgiveness of sins, just as the apostles had been taught by the Lord himself (see Acts 2:36–38).

So the question is not about tradition or personal heritage. It is this:

Have you obeyed the gospel of Jesus Christ? Have you entered into discipleship the way Jesus described it—through faith, baptism, and obedience?

If the answer is "yes," then rejoice and continue walking in it with all your heart.

If the answer is uncertain—or even "no"—then today may be the day to begin again, not by emotion or assumption, but by conviction, by Scripture, and by the Spirit.

The Third Decision point

The Turning Point: Who Will Teach You? Who Will Baptize You?

At some point in the journey of every would-be disciple, the questions cease to be theoretical. They become personal. It is not enough to admire the teachings of Jesus or agree in principle with the Scriptures. The call of the gospel demands a response that involves real people, real obedience, and real decisions.

So ask yourself plainly:

Who has taught you this message of Jesus—not a version of it, not a tradition about it, but the message as it was passed down by the apostles?

And just as important:

Who is going to baptize you, in accordance with Scripture and Jesus' command?

This may well be the most difficult decision on the path to salvation—not because it is unclear, but because it is so concrete. It requires humility. It requires surrender. And it requires a willingness to let go of whatever pride, fear, or assumption might be standing in the way.

In moments like this, we each find ourselves reflected in the lives of others from Scripture:

• Are you like Naaman—the commander of armies, the powerful man who balked at the simplicity of God's instruction? When told to wash in the Jordan to be cleansed of his leprosy, he was angry. "Are not the rivers of Damascus better?" he asked (2 Kings 5:12). But when he humbled himself and obeyed, he was healed.

• Or are you like Saul of Tarsus—a devoutly religious man, zealous for God, yet blind to the very Messiah he claimed to serve? When confronted by Jesus, he asked, "What shall I do, Lord?" (Acts 22:10). And the answer was not mystical—it was concrete: go, and you will be told. And in that city, a disciple named Ananias taught him, and said: "What are you waiting for? Get up, be baptized and wash your sins away, calling on his name" (Acts 22:16). Saul obeyed—and became Paul.

- Or, heartbreakingly, are you like the rich young man—eager, searching, even reverent—but unwilling to let go of a lifestyle, an identity, or a comfort zone to follow Jesus fully? "He went away sad, because he had great wealth" (Mark 10:22). He believed in Jesus, but he would not follow.

This moment is no less real for you and me.

Will we humble ourselves and be taught—not by feelings or tradition, but by a disciple who knows and lives the gospel of Jesus Christ?

Will we be baptized in the name of the Father, the Son, and the Holy Spirit, as Jesus instructed—not symbolically, but obediently, in faith for the forgiveness of sins and entry into new life?

Salvation is not abstract. It happens through real obedience to the real Jesus—who sends real people to teach, to guide, to baptize.

So then, if you have not yet responded to the gospel in this way, the next decision becomes urgent:

Who will teach you? Who will walk with you? Who will baptize you according to the Word of Christ?

That's not just a logistical question. It is a spiritual crossroads. And how you answer it may well shape your eternity.

False Doctrines

What Must I Do to Be Saved? – One True Answer, Many False Roads

There is no more important question a human being can ask:

"What must I do to be saved?"

The tragedy of our time—and indeed of many centuries—is not that this question lacks an answer, but that the one true answer has often been obscured, distorted, or replaced. Not by accident, but because:

• Some have failed to rightly handle the Word of God.

• Others have given themselves over to myths, distractions, and self-importance.

• Many have refused to repent from hypocrisy and cling instead to the comfort of compromise.

• And countless souls have chosen to listen not to sound doctrine, but only to what their itching ears wish to hear.

This is not a new problem. Paul warned of it in his letters. Jesus confronted it in his ministry. And still today, the church is not immune. There are false answers to the question of salvation, and these lead people not into life, but into deception.

As such, we must speak plainly. False teachings on salvation generally fall into three broad categories—each one cutting the roots of the gospel and offering something other than the foundation Christ laid.

1. Requiring Old Testament Practices as Conditions for Salvation

Some still insist that certain elements of the Mosaic law—circumcision, dietary rules, Sabbath regulations, or Jewish ritual observances—must be kept in order to be a "true" Christian. But this is precisely the controversy the apostles addressed in the book of Acts and in Paul's letters (see Galatians, Romans).

Christ has fulfilled the Law (Matthew 5:17), and salvation is no longer through the covenantal symbols of the old age, but through faith in the Messiah and obedience to his teaching. To add to that gospel is to fall from grace (Galatians 5:4).

2. An Incomplete Gospel – Half of the Message

Others preach part of the message—faith, but not repentance; belief, but not baptism; grace, but not discipleship. Jesus never invited people to accept a portion of his teaching. He said:

"Teach them to obey everything I have commanded you."

(Matthew 28:20)

An incomplete gospel may feel comfortable, but it is not the gospel that saves. If we are to follow Jesus, we must receive the full message—his call to believe, repent, be baptized, and follow him as Lord.

3. Man-Made Doctrines That Supplant Jesus' Commands

Perhaps the most common danger today is the elevation of man-made theology or denominational traditions over the plain instructions of Christ. When systems and institutions begin to replace or reinterpret the commands of Jesus, we are left with religious forms that have no spiritual power.

Jesus spoke plainly of this:

"Why do you call me, 'Lord, Lord,' and do not do what I say?

I will show you what he is like who comes to me and hears my words and puts them into practice..." ~ (Luke 6:46–47)

He compares the obedient disciple to a man who dug deep and laid his foundation on the rock—that rock being Jesus' teaching. But the one who hears and does not obey is like a man building on bare ground. When the flood comes, "its destruction was complete." (Luke 6:49)

And as he warned with another parable:

"Can a blind man lead a blind man? Will they not both fall into a pit?"
(Luke 6:39)

This is the spiritual condition of much of the modern church—blind leaders guiding blind followers into theological confusion, cultural compromise, or emotional religion devoid of biblical obedience.

Only One Foundation

To ask, "What must I do to be saved?" and receive the true answer, you must return to the words of Jesus and the gospel preached by his apostles. Not the gospel of partial truth. Not the gospel of law-keeping. Not the gospel of human tradition.

But the gospel that calls us to hear his words, obey them, and build our lives upon them.

For only this gospel will stand when the floods come—and they will.

Only One Gospel, Many Roads: A Warning Against False Doctrines

The question "What must I do to be saved?" has only one answer, rooted in the teaching and example of Jesus, affirmed by the apostles, and recorded in the Scriptures. And yet across the centuries, many have offered competing answers—built not on the words of Christ, but on human speculation, religious invention, and misplaced zeal.

This did not begin in our time. From the earliest days of the church, there were those who twisted the gospel, not necessarily out of malice, but out of misunderstanding, fear, and the desire to control. Denominations and splinter movements have often been born not of obedience to Jesus, but of anxieties about grace and the compulsion to improve upon God's simplicity.

We must take Paul's counsel seriously:

"Examine yourselves to see whether you are in the faith" (2 Corinthians 13:5).

For 2,000 years removed from Jesus' voice, the only safe path is to return again—and again—to what is written.

1. The Error of Adding Old Testament Regulations

The first great crisis in the early church did not come from outside persecution, but from within—from those who insisted that Gentile converts must still obey the laws of Moses to be saved. The issue reached such a critical point that the apostles themselves gathered in Jerusalem to settle it (Acts 15).

"Why do you put God to the test," Peter asked, "by placing a yoke on the neck of the disciples that neither our fathers nor we have been able to bear?" (Acts 15:10)

This wasn't a trivial issue. It was a matter of salvation. Peter, Paul, and the other apostles made it clear: we are saved by grace through faith in Jesus, not by keeping the Mosaic law. To add circumcision, dietary codes, or festivals as requirements for salvation was not an enhancement—it was a betrayal of the gospel itself.

And yet today, the same error persists. Entire traditions have emerged insisting on a return to the sabbath, Jewish feasts, or Old Testament rituals as if they complete the gospel. But Paul wrote:

"Let no one judge you... about eating and drinking, or with regard to a festival, a new moon, or a sabbath. These are a shadow of the things to come, but the substance belongs to Christ."
(Colossians 2:16-17)

To insist on the shadow after the reality has come is to miss the heart of the gospel.

2. Denominational Errors Born of Misreading and Mysticism

In the 1800s, a seaman who found Christ in the Methodist tradition began teaching speculative doctrines about the return of Jesus, angelic visitations, and the sabbath as a requirement for true worship. His movement grew into a full denomination—fervent, devout, yet tragically misled.

Paul's words to the Colossians echo like a warning across time:

"Let no one disqualify you, insisting on asceticism and worship of angels, going on in detail about visions... not holding fast to the Head, from whom the whole body grows..."
(Colossians 2:18–19)
Even in the earliest churches, mysticism and fascination with the supernatural threatened to divert people from Christ. And when paired with legalism—rules about food, days, and rituals—it became a false gospel.

Christ is enough. In him, Paul says, "the fullness of the Godhead dwells bodily," and in him we are "made complete" (Colossians 2:9–10). Adding anything to Christ does not deepen the gospel—it destroys it.

The Real Danger of False Doctrines

False teachings do not always appear sinister. They often come wrapped in zeal, dressed in Scripture, and led by people who sincerely believe they are honoring God. But Jesus' words remain:

"Why do you call me, 'Lord, Lord,' and do not do what I say?" (Luke 6:46)

To build a life, or a church, on anything other than obedience to Jesus' actual words is like building a house with no foundation. It may look strong, even beautiful, but when the flood comes—and it always does—"its destruction will be complete" (Luke 6:49).

A Call to Personal Responsibility and Scriptural Integrity

You and I are not called to a denomination.

We are not called to a movement.

We are not called to a personality.

We are called to Christ—and to his Word.

In an age of confusion, compromise, and countless religious paths, our only hope is to do what the earliest Christians did: open the Scriptures, examine our lives, and demand of ourselves the kind of obedience Jesus called for from the beginning.

So then, as the prophet once asked, we must ask again:

"To whom shall we go? You have the words of eternal life."
(John 6:68)

And to him we must go—no matter the cost, no matter how many turn away.

2) The Myth of "Once Saved, Always Saved": A Warning from Scripture

Among the most dangerous distortions of the gospel today is the teaching that once a person is "saved," their salvation is eternally secure—regardless of how they live, whether they persevere, or whether they continue in obedience to Christ. While this may offer a kind of emotional comfort, it does not reflect the full witness of Scripture. In fact, it runs directly counter to the very words of Jesus and the sober warnings of the apostles.

Let us begin with Jesus himself. As crowds gathered from town after town, he taught them a parable—not merely for reflection, but for self-examination and decision:

"A farmer went out to sow his seed..."
(Luke 8:4–15)
The parable of the sower reveals that not all who receive the Word endure. Some receive it with joy, but they have no root—"they believe for a while, but in the time of testing they fall away." Others let the Word be choked by the cares and pleasures of life. Only those who "hear the word, retain it, and by persevering produce a crop" are truly faithful.

This is not theoretical. It is Jesus' own description of discipleship. And it dismantles the illusion that belief at one point in time guarantees salvation, regardless of what follows. "They believe for a while..." Jesus says—and still fall away. Faith must be persevering to be saving.

The Warning from Hebrews: A Call to Daily Faithfulness

The writer of Hebrews speaks not to outsiders but to Christians— to baptized believers who have begun the journey. And yet, he warns with unmistakable clarity:

"Take care, brothers, lest there be in any of you an evil, unbelieving heart, leading you to fall away from the living God." ~ (Hebrews 3:12)

The message is urgent: faith is not a past decision but a present commitment. He goes on:

"We have come to share in Christ, if indeed we hold our original confidence firm to the end."
(Hebrews 3:14)

The pattern is unmistakable—those who began the exodus out of Egypt with Moses, who experienced God's mighty deliverance, still perished in the wilderness. Not because they never believed, but because they ceased to trust and obey.

Paul's Message: Salvation Means a New Life, Not a Free Pass

Paul, writing in Romans 6, makes it equally clear: to be "saved" is to be buried with Christ in baptism and raised to walk in newness of life. The very image of baptism is one of death and resurrection—a total transformation of self.

"Shall we go on sinning so that grace may increase? By no means!"
(Romans 6:1)

"Do you not know that all of us who were baptized into Christ Jesus were baptized into his death?" (Romans 6:3)

Paul's conclusion is not that grace excuses ongoing sin, but that grace empowers transformation. We are to "consider ourselves dead to sin but alive to God in Christ Jesus" (Romans 6:11). If we return to sin, we undo the very act of dying with Christ. Salvation is not static; it is a life lived in ongoing faithfulness and surrender.

False Assurance vs. True Obedience

The doctrine of "once saved, always saved" can create a false assurance that leads people to ignore their spiritual condition. It removes the urgency of discipleship. It dulls the call to obedience. It turns grace into license.

Jesus, however, was never vague:

"Why do you call me, 'Lord, Lord,' and not do what I say?"

(Luke 6:46)

Those who hear but do not practice his words are building on sand. The storm will come. And the house will fall.

The True Gospel: Salvation Requires Endurance

The early church understood that salvation was not just about beginning the race but finishing it. Faith, baptism, and repentance were the doorways into life—but obedience, perseverance, and the ongoing work of the Spirit were the path.

"By your endurance you will gain your lives." ~ (Luke 21:19)

So then, the question is not, "Were you saved once?" but rather,

"Are you still walking in Christ, obeying his word, dying to self, and bearing fruit?"

If so, continue in that grace.

If not, the invitation remains: Come back. Repent. Walk again.

3) "Pray Jesus into Your Heart"? The Error of the Pharisee

One of the most widespread yet unbiblical ideas in contemporary Christianity is the notion that a person is "saved" by praying Jesus into their heart. It is often spoken with sincerity and good intention, but it is nowhere taught in Scripture. It is the product of a modern misunderstanding of biblical faith—what we might call a theology of convenience, where salvation is reduced to a moment of emotional assent, detached from the call to obedient discipleship.

This idea, though sounding spiritual, bears resemblance to what we might call the error of the Pharisee: clinging to religious forms while missing the heart of God's message.

Context Is Everything: What Jesus Actually Told Nicodemus

Often, this teaching is propped up by verses like John 3:16 and Romans 10:9–11, plucked from their context and repurposed to support a theology Jesus never preached.

But let's listen carefully to the full conversation in John 3. Nicodemus, a Pharisee and teacher of Israel, comes to Jesus at night. He knows Jesus is from God—"no one could perform the signs you are doing if God were not with him." But Jesus responds with something shocking:

"Very truly I tell you, no one can see the kingdom of God unless they are born again."
(John 3:3)

Nicodemus is baffled. Jesus explains that this new birth requires two things: water and the Spirit (John 3:5). This is no vague spiritual metaphor. Jesus is referring directly to what Nicodemus, as a teacher of the Law, should have understood—the preparatory baptism of repentance proclaimed by John, and the coming rebirth through the Holy Spirit.

Later in the same passage, Jesus references his own future death:

"Just as Moses lifted up the snake in the wilderness, so the Son of Man must be lifted up..." (John 3:14)

This is not Jesus giving Nicodemus a "sinner's prayer." It is Jesus explaining what it will cost him to bring salvation, and how those who believe in him must respond—not simply with belief, but with transformation through water and Spirit.

The Danger of Lazy Contextomy

To "pray Jesus into your heart" is the result of what might be called lazy contextomy—ripping verses out of context and building an entire doctrine on fragments.

Romans 10:9–11, another commonly cited passage, is often used to support this theology:

"If you declare with your mouth, 'Jesus is Lord,' and believe in your heart that God raised him from the dead, you will be saved."
But Paul is not laying out a simplistic formula. He is writing to baptized believers in Rome, summarizing the heart of the gospel: allegiance to Jesus as Lord and trust in his resurrection power. Confession here is not a one-time utterance, but a declaration of loyalty—a pledge of lifelong faithfulness within the larger story of God's salvation through Israel and fulfilled in Jesus the Messiah.

John the Baptist and the Rejection of Repentance

Jesus' rebuke of Nicodemus also alludes to Israel's rejection of John's baptism—a baptism of repentance for the forgiveness of sins (Mark 1:4). John's mission was foretold by the prophets: he would come "in the spirit of Elijah," preparing the way for the Lord (Isaiah 40; Malachi 3–4).

Those who rejected John's baptism were, in essence, rejecting God's call to repent. And as Luke records:

"But the Pharisees and the lawyers rejected the purpose of God for themselves, not having been baptized by him."
(Luke 7:30)

To be born of water and Spirit, then, was not a mystical idea—it was a call to real repentance and public obedience. Jesus was telling Nicodemus—and through him, us—that salvation involves real transformation, not just religious acknowledgment.

True Salvation: Obedience, Not Convenience

Salvation in the New Testament is not accomplished by whispering a private prayer in a moment of emotion. It is the result of hearing the gospel, repenting, being baptized in the name of Jesus Christ for the forgiveness of sins, and receiving the Holy Spirit (Acts 2:38).

Jesus never said, *"Accept me into your heart."* He said, *"Take up your cross and follow me."* He didn't ask for admiration—he called for **obedience**.

So let us be clear:

- There is no salvation apart from obedience to the gospel.
- There is no shortcut around repentance and baptism.
- There is no "sinner's prayer" in the teaching of Jesus or the practice of the apostles.

Instead, there is one Lord, one faith, one baptism (Ephesians 4:5).

There is the Word made flesh, calling us into a new life by dying with him in baptism and rising to walk in the Spirit.

The only way in is the way he gave us.

And it is enough.

3) "Pray Jesus into Your Heart"? – A Gospel Without Obedience Is No Gospel at All

One of the most widely accepted yet unbiblical doctrines in the modern church is the idea that one becomes a Christian simply by "praying Jesus into your heart." While it may sound spiritual and comforting, this teaching is entirely absent from the Scriptures, and dangerously misleading.

It is a theology built not on the teachings of Jesus or the apostles, but on centuries of simplification, emotionalism, and contextomy—the practice of extracting verses from their biblical context and reshaping them into doctrines Jesus never gave.

The Misuse of John 3 and Romans 10

Two passages are frequently cited to defend this teaching: John 3:16 and Romans 10:8–11. But neither of these, read in context, supports the idea that salvation happens through a personal prayer alone, apart from baptism, repentance, and obedient discipleship.

In John 3, Jesus is not laying out a method of salvation. He is speaking with Nicodemus, a Pharisee and teacher of Israel, who should have known from the Scriptures what it means to be prepared for the coming Messiah. Jesus tells him:

"No one can enter the kingdom of God unless they are born of water and the Spirit." ~ (John 3:5)

This is a direct reference to the baptism of repentance preached by John the Baptist and to the new birth that the Spirit brings. Jesus is saying that those who truly believe must respond by obeying God's revealed call to repentance, baptism, and Spirit-led transformation—just as those who looked upon the bronze serpent in the wilderness obeyed Moses and lived.

John 3:16 follows this as a statement of what God's love has done: sent His Son, so that all who believe—in the biblical sense of trust-filled obedience—might be saved. But belief, in Scripture, is never abstract. It is always expressed in action.

Likewise, Romans 10:9–10 is not a magical incantation for salvation. Paul is addressing believers in Rome who had already been baptized into Christ (Romans 6), reminding them of the heart of the gospel: confession of Jesus as Lord, and belief in his resurrection. It is a summary of kingdom allegiance, not a standalone ritual.

And immediately after these verses, Paul asks a series of rhetorical questions:

"How, then, can they call on the one they have not believed in? And how can they believe in the one of whom they have not heard?"

(Romans 10:14)

This echoes Paul's own story: he did not figure it out on his own. He had to hear the message, be confronted, and obey.

Paul's Conversion: The Pattern of Obedience

Paul's transformation on the road to Damascus is one of the clearest counterexamples to the "sinner's prayer" teaching. He encountered Jesus personally, was blinded, and spent three days fasting and praying. And yet, it was not until a disciple—Ananias—came to him with a clear word from the Lord that Paul understood what he must do:

"And now, what are you waiting for? Get up, be baptized and wash your sins away, calling on his name."
(Acts 22:16)

Even Paul, with a direct encounter from Jesus, was not saved through prayer alone, but through obedience—submission to the gospel preached by a disciple, baptism for the forgiveness of sins, and the reception of the Holy Spirit. The Ethiopian eunuch, Cornelius, Lydia, the jailer in Philippi—every salvation story in Acts follows the same pattern: faith, repentance, baptism, obedience.

Salvation Cannot Be Rewritten

Let us be crystal clear:

Jesus never said, "Pray and invite me into your heart."

He said, *"If anyone would come after me, let him deny himself, take up his cross daily, and follow me."* ~ (Luke 9:23)

And again:

"Why do you call me, 'Lord, Lord,' and not do what I say?" ~ (Luke 6:46)

To build our hope of salvation on anything less than Jesus' actual command is to build our house on sand. The foundation is not emotion, not tradition, not sincerity—it is obedient faith grounded in the gospel, confirmed by baptism, and lived out by the Spirit.

The gospel is not a personal invention. It is the announced good news of what God has done in Jesus, and how we must respond. That response, laid out by Jesus himself and proclaimed by his apostles, is this:

- Hear the message of the kingdom.

- Believe in the risen Lord.

- Repent of your sins.

- Be baptized in the name of Jesus for the forgiveness of sins.

- Receive the Holy Spirit.

- Walk in obedience to Christ's teachings.

There is no other gospel. Anything less—however popular, however emotional, however well-meaning—is not the gospel of the New Testament.

Let us not be among those who say "Lord, Lord" yet do not do what he says. Let us dig deep. Lay our lives on the rock. And follow him, fully, faithfully, and truly.

4) "Anyone Saved Speaks in Tongues"? Clarifying the Gift, Correcting the Error

One of the more recent and emotionally charged doctrines in some streams of modern Christianity is the belief that speaking in tongues is the necessary evidence of salvation. It is often taught, implicitly or explicitly, that unless one speaks in tongues, one has not truly received the Holy Spirit and therefore is not yet saved.

Yet when we look seriously at the New Testament—in its full narrative and theological context—we find that this claim is not only unsupported, but deeply misleading. It fails to understand the purpose of tongues, their role in the story of the early church, and the way the Holy Spirit truly works in the life of a believer.

Tongues in the New Testament: Three Key Moments

There are three major scenes where speaking in tongues occurs in the New Testament:

1. Acts 2 – Pentecost:

The apostles, having waited in Jerusalem as Jesus commanded, receive the Holy Spirit. They begin to speak in other known languages, and Jews from every nation hear the message in their own tongues. This is not ecstatic or unintelligible speech—it is miraculous translation, a reversal of Babel, signaling the arrival of the kingdom and the birth of the church.

2. Acts 10 – Cornelius and the Gentiles:

When Peter preaches to the household of Cornelius, the Holy Spirit falls upon them before baptism—clearly by God's initiative—to confirm that Gentiles, too, are being welcomed into the people of God. Tongues serve as a sign, not a requirement. Peter responds by immediately commanding them to be baptized (Acts 10:48).

3. Acts 19 – Disciples of John in Ephesus:

Paul encounters men who have been baptized only into John's baptism. When he explains the gospel of Jesus, they are baptized in the name of the Lord Jesus. Paul lays hands on them, and they receive the Holy Spirit and speak in tongues—once again, a special confirmation tied to apostolic authority.

In each of these moments, tongues are not a universal command or expectation. They are fulfillments of prophecy—signposts marking key transitions in the unfolding plan of God: from Jews to Gentiles, from John's preparation to Jesus' kingdom, from confusion to clarity.

Paul and the Church at Corinth: A Cautionary Tale

The only church where tongues become a widespread issue is Corinth. But far from encouraging their obsession with the gift, Paul corrects them sharply:

"In the church I would rather speak five intelligible words to instruct others than ten thousand words in a tongue." ~ 1 Corinthians 14:19

And again:

"Tongues, then, are a sign, not for believers but for unbelievers..."
(1 Corinthians 14:22)

Here Paul is quoting from the prophets to show that unintelligible speech serves not to edify the church, but to fulfill Scripture's warning that a people who will not listen will hear foreign tongues—and still not understand (see Isaiah 28:11–12).

Tongues are not evidence of salvation.

They are a sign, a warning, and at times a gift—used for the building up of the church, never for status, and certainly never as a condition for new birth.

Receiving the Spirit: Not Tongues, But Baptism and Faith

Peter is clear on the day of Pentecost:

"Repent and be baptized, every one of you, in the name of Jesus Christ for the forgiveness of your sins. And you will receive the gift of the Holy Spirit."
(Acts 2:38)

This promise is universal. It is for everyone who obeys the gospel. The Holy Spirit is received at baptism, when one turns in faith to the risen Jesus—not through a second blessing, not through emotional experience, and not by tongues.

Even Simon the magician understood that the miraculous gifts came only through apostolic laying on of hands—not as a universal sign of salvation, but as a unique witness to the gospel's expansion through apostolic authority (Acts 8:18–20).

The Core Error: Making a Sign into a Standard

The danger in saying "everyone saved speaks in tongues" is that it places human expectations above divine instruction. It turns what was occasional and miraculous into something mandatory and mechanical—and in doing so, it distorts the very heart of the gospel.

Tongues are never commanded. They are never presented as the litmus test for genuine faith. And they are not the normative experience of those who come to Christ. The normative response is what Jesus, Peter, and Paul all preached: repentance, baptism, and a life of obedience filled with the Spirit.

Conclusion: Back to the Foundation

As Jesus himself said:

"Why do you call me, 'Lord, Lord,' and do not do what I say?"
(Luke 6:46)

The true mark of salvation is obedience to his words—not emotional experience, not spiritual gifts, not inherited tradition. It is a heart turned to God, a life laid down in baptism, and a walk of faith that reflects the character of Christ.

The Spirit of God is not proved by spectacle, but by transformation.

Let us return, then, not to what excites the crowd, but to what was written from the beginning.

5) No One Is Saved by Their Own Good Deeds—But Neither Is Anyone Saved Without Obedience

It must be said at the outset—and said clearly: no one is saved by their own good deeds. The gospel of Jesus Christ is not about moral achievement or spiritual performance. Salvation is the unmerited gift of God, extended to us through the death and resurrection of the Messiah, and received by faith.

But then comes the vital question: What kind of faith?

This is where so many have lost their way. Faith has too often been reduced to mental agreement, or to a feeling, or to a verbal affirmation made in a moment of emotion. But this is not the faith Jesus described, nor the apostles preached, nor the Scriptures bear witness to.

As the prophet Jeremiah reminds us:

"The heart is deceitful above all things and beyond cure. Who can understand it?"
(Jeremiah 17:9)

In other words, it is easy to say we have faith. But what does that faith look like when examined by the light of God's Word?

Faith Without Obedience Is Not Faith at All

James, the brother of Jesus and one of the most influential leaders of the early church, writes with crystal clarity:

"What good is it, my brothers and sisters, if someone claims to have faith but has no deeds? Can such faith save them?"
(James 2:14)

The answer, of course, is no. Faith that does not result in obedient action is not saving faith—it is illusion. As James continues:

"You believe that there is one God. Good! Even the demons believe that—and shudder."
(James 2:19)

Faith must be more than doctrinal correctness. It must be embodied trust, evidenced by a life that has turned toward God. James cites Abraham and Rahab—both of whom demonstrated their trust in God by what they did. Their deeds did not earn salvation. But they confirmed the authenticity of their faith.

"As the body without the spirit is dead, so faith without deeds is dead."
(James 2:26)

Paul and James Agree: Faith Is Trust That Obeys

Some have wrongly assumed that James and Paul were at odds on this point, but that reflects a misunderstanding of both. Paul, writing to the Romans, is unequivocal: we are not saved by the works of the law. But he is equally emphatic that faith is not passive.

"Shall we go on sinning so that grace may increase? By no means!"
(Romans 6:1-2)

Paul goes on to explain that believers are baptized into Christ's death and raised to live a new life. Baptism is not a symbolic afterthought—it is the moment of dying to the old self, being united with Jesus, and beginning a life of actual transformation (Romans 6:3–14).

And just a few verses later, Paul says:

"Thanks be to God that, though you used to be slaves to sin, you have come to obey from the heart the pattern of teaching that has now claimed your allegiance."
(Romans 6:17)

Obedience is not the opposite of faith. It is faith's fullest expression.

The Flood Analogy: Faith Made Visible in Action

Consider the man drowning in a flood. A rescuer comes and says, "Climb on my back—I will carry you to safety." The man may say he trusts the rescuer. But his real faith is shown by whether or not he climbs on.

So it is with Jesus. Faith is not faith unless it climbs on. Unless it acts. Unless it follows. Unless it submits.

This is why Jesus said:

"Not everyone who says to me, 'Lord, Lord,' will enter the kingdom of heaven, but only the one who does the will of my Father who is in heaven."
(Matthew 7:21)

True Faith Produces a New Kind of Life

Faith is not about achieving perfection. It is about living a new life in the power of the Spirit—a life marked by repentance, love, generosity, justice, humility, and mission. The rich man who ignored Lazarus at his gate had religion, but no righteousness. His lack of compassion revealed the absence of true faith (Luke 16:19–31).

Hebrews 11 presents the ultimate roll call of faith—not as abstract belief, but as radical obedience to the call of Heaven:

- Noah built an ark.

- Abraham left his country.

- Moses refused the luxury of Pharaoh's palace.

- Rahab risked her life to protect God's people.

In every case, faith worked itself out through obedient action. That is biblical faith.

So Then, What Must We Say?

No one is saved by good deeds apart from Christ.

But no one is saved into Christ who refuses to obey him.

Faith that does not respond to Jesus' message—faith that does not begin with repentance, baptism, and a new way of life—is not faith that saves.

Let us then reject both errors:

- The error of legalism, that we earn salvation.

- And the error of license, that faith excuses us from obedience.

Instead, let us embrace the full gospel:

By grace, through faith, expressed in obedience, we are saved.

And in Christ, we are made new to live the life of the kingdom—here and now, and forever.

When all is said and done

When all is said and done, let us be utterly clear: attending church—whether on Sunday or Saturday or any day of the week—is not what brings salvation. Neither is speaking in tongues, nor all-night prayer meetings, nor even passionate engagement in religious activities. Important as communal worship and spiritual disciplines may be in the life of the believer, they are not the foundation of salvation.

Jesus did not go to the cross, did not rise from the grave, simply to inaugurate a new set of religious routines. He died and rose so that we might be delivered from sin and death, become his disciples, and walk in faithful obedience, transformed by the Spirit and living out his mission in the world.

At the heart of this calling is what Jesus himself taught: believe in him, trust him, and obey him—beginning with his final instruction to be baptized and to follow him in a life of love, service, and faithful witness to others.

There is perhaps no parable that strikes this note with greater force than the one recorded in Luke 16:19–31. Jesus tells of a rich man, clothed in purple and feasting in luxury, while a poor man named Lazarus lies at his gate, covered in sores and longing for crumbs. When both men die, their roles are reversed: Lazarus is comforted in the presence of Abraham, and the rich man is in torment. He begs for relief, even for someone to return from the dead to warn his brothers. But the reply comes:

"They have Moses and the prophets; let them hear them."

"If they do not listen to Moses and the prophets, neither will they be convinced even if someone rises from the dead."
(Luke 16:29, 31)

This is not merely a tale about the afterlife. It is a prophetic indictment. Jesus is calling us to listen to the Scriptures—not merely read them, but to hear them and obey. His warning lands with particular weight: the man had the Scriptures, just as we do. And so we have no excuse for living lives that ignore the needs of others or treat religious piety as a substitute for compassion.

Jesus doubles down on this in Matthew 7. There he says, pointedly:

"Enter through the narrow gate... small is the gate and narrow the road that leads to life, and only a few find it."
(Matthew 7:13-14)

And he continues:

"Not everyone who says to me, 'Lord, Lord,' will enter the kingdom of heaven, but only the one who does the will of my Father who is in heaven."
(Matthew 7:21)

Many, Jesus says, will claim great religious achievements—prophecy, exorcism, miraculous signs. But none of that is the measure of discipleship. He will respond:

"I never knew you. Away from me, you evildoers!"
(Matthew 7:23)

The key is not spiritual spectacle, but obedience—a life built on the solid rock of hearing Jesus' words and putting them into practice (Matthew 7:24–27).

And so we must ask: Is our life built on that rock? Are we simply going through the motions of religion, while ignoring the heart of Jesus' message? Have we mistaken church involvement for covenant faithfulness?

To trust Jesus means to obey Jesus. It means to take his words seriously, to reject the path of performance or empty religious tradition, and to walk instead in the newness of life that flows from his cross and resurrection.

As James, the brother of our Lord, wrote with pastoral urgency:

"Faith by itself, if it is not accompanied by action, is dead... Show me your faith without deeds, and I will show you my faith by my deeds." (James 2:17-18)

James isn't opposing Paul's teaching on grace—he's clarifying it. True faith is not passive. It is embodied. It acts. It repents. It obeys. James' letter is not merely theological reflection; it is a call to courage—to a discipleship that does not rest in ritual but risks everything in obedience to Jesus.

Let me, then, urge you—as Jesus urged those in his own day—to listen. To examine not only what you believe, but how you live. To recognize that the path is narrow not because it is exclusive, but because it demands everything of us. Not perfection, but allegiance. Not just admiration, but submission. Not just emotion, but faithfulness.

Religious appearance is no substitute for kingdom obedience. Jesus is not looking for fans—he is calling disciples.

And so, let us return again to his final instruction—baptize, teach, obey—and walk in it with joy. For there, and only there, we find the life that truly is life.

Letter written by James, a disciple of Christ

Let me offer a word of encouragement through the letter of James, a servant of God and of the Lord Jesus the Messiah—a letter as rich in wisdom as it is urgent in its call to obedience.

James writes to the scattered tribes, those living as God's people in exile among the nations, with a message that rings with the clarity of the prophets and the insight of one who walked alongside Jesus himself.

"Count it all joy," he says, when you face trials of many kinds, because faith under pressure produces endurance. And endurance, when it completes its work, shapes the kind of character God desires—a life whole and lacking nothing (James 1:2–4). But if you lack wisdom? Ask! Ask in faith, not with a divided heart, because God is generous to all who truly seek him (1:5–8).

James offers a sweeping critique of false religiosity—the kind that professes godliness while leaving the vulnerable unserved and the heart unchanged. Real faith, true discipleship, is not merely hearing the Word, but doing it (1:22). To hear without obeying, he says, is like looking in a mirror and walking away forgetting your face.

And what does true religion look like? James makes it plain: to care for widows and orphans in their distress, and to remain unstained by the world (1:27). It is a faith that moves toward others in mercy, not away in judgment. It is a life that reflects the character of the God who has no shadow of turning (1:17).

He warns sternly against favoritism—a sin not only of injustice, but of theological contradiction. To honor the rich while dishonoring the poor is to forget the very heart of the gospel: that God has chosen the poor in the eyes of the world to be rich in faith and heirs of the kingdom (2:5).

James will not let us take refuge in belief alone. "Even the demons believe," he writes, "and tremble" (2:19). What counts is a faith that is made complete by action. Abraham believed God—yes—but it was when he offered up Isaac that his faith was shown to be genuine (2:21–22). Faith without works is dead. Not weakened, not immature—dead (2:26).

From there, James turns to the tongue, that small but powerful member of the body, capable of great blessing and grave destruction. "With it we bless the Lord and Father, and with it we curse people made in his image. My brothers and sisters, this should not be" (3:9–10).

The wisdom from above, James says, is "pure, peace-loving, considerate, submissive, full of mercy and good fruit, impartial and sincere" (3:17). Where envy and selfish ambition rule, there is disorder. But the fruit of righteousness is sown in peace by those who make peace.

He speaks as well of quarrels, pride, and the danger of becoming a friend of the world. "Submit yourselves, then, to God. Resist the devil, and he will flee from you. Draw near to God, and he will draw near to you" (4:7–8). And again, he reminds them: do not judge your neighbor, do not boast about tomorrow, do not place trust in riches that will rot and fade.

But then—a pastoral turn. "Be patient," he says, "until the coming of the Lord." Like a farmer waiting for rain, establish your hearts. Do not grumble against one another. Remember the prophets who suffered, remember Job. And above all: let your "yes" be yes and your "no" be no (5:7–12).

He closes with a vision of the community grounded in prayer and mutual care. "Is anyone among you suffering? Let them pray. Is anyone cheerful? Let them sing. Is anyone sick? Call for the elders... The prayer of faith will save the sick" (5:13–15). And in perhaps one of the most beautiful expressions of the church's vocation:

"Whoever brings back a sinner from wandering will save their soul from death and cover a multitude of sins" (5:20).

This is James, servant of the Lord Jesus: calling us to a faith that acts, a wisdom that submits, a church that heals, and a people who live as if Jesus really is Lord.

Appendix

On the Physical Death of Jesus Christ

William Edwards, M.D. (Anatomic Pathology, Mayo Clinic), Wesley Gabel, M.Div., and Floyd Hosmer, M.S, AMI, published the results of their investigation "On the Physical Death of Jesus Christ" Journal of the American Medical Association (JAMA) 1986; 255:1455-1463

Jesus of Nazareth underwent Jewish and Roman trials, was flogged, and was sentenced to death by crucifixion. The scourging produced deep stripe-like lacerations and appreciable blood loss, and it probably set the stage for hypovolemic shock, as evidenced by the fact that Jesus was too weakened to carry the crossbar (patibulum) to Golgotha. At the site of crucifixion, his wrists were nailed to the patibulum and, after the patibulum was lifted onto the upright post (stipes), his feet were nailed to the stipes. The major pathophysiologic effect of crucifixion was an interference with normal respirations. Accordingly, death resulted primarily from hypovolemic shock and exhaustion asphyxia. Jesus' death was ensured by the thrust of a soldier's spear into his side. Modern medical interpretation of the historical evidence indicates that Jesus was dead when taken down from the cross.

THE LIFE and teachings of Jesus of Nazareth have formed the basis for a major world religion (Christianity), have appreciably influenced the course of human history, and, by virtue of a compassionate attitude toward the sick, also have contributed to the development of modern medicine. The eminence of Jesus as a historical figure and the suffering and controversy associated with his death have stimulated us to investigate, in an interdisciplinary manner, the circumstances surrounding his crucifixion. Accordingly, it is our intent to present not a theological treatise but rather a medically and historically accurate account of the physical death of the one called Jesus Christ.

SOURCES

The source material concerning Christ's death comprises a body of literature and not a physical body or its skeletal remains. Accordingly, the credibility of any discussion of Jesus' death will be determined primarily by the credibility of one's sources. For this review, the source material includes the writings of ancient Christian and non-Christian authors, the writings of modern authors, and the Shroud of Turin. Using the legal-historical method of scientific investigation, scholars have established the reliability and accuracy of the ancient manuscripts.

The most extensive and detailed description of the life and death of Jesus are to be found in the New Testament gospels of Matthew, Mark, Luke, and John. The other 23 books of the New Testament support, but do not expand on the details recorded in the gospels. Contemporary Christian, Jewish, and Roman authors provide additional insight concerning the first-century Jewish and Roman legal systems and the details of scourging and crucifixion. Seneca, Livy, Plutarch, and others refer to crucifixion practices in their works. Specifically, Jesus (or his crucifixion) is mentioned by the Roman historians Cornelius Tacitus, Pliny the Younger, and Suetonius, by non-Roman historians Thallus and Phlegon, by the satirist Lucian of Samosata, by the Jewish Talmud, and by the Jewish historian Flavius Josephus, although the authenticity of portions of the latter is problematic.

The Shroud of Turin is considered by many to represent the actual burial cloth of Jesus, and several publications concerning the medical aspects of his death draw conclusions from this assumption. The Shroud of Turin and recent archaeological findings provide valuable information concerning Roman crucifixion practices. The interpretations of modern writers, based on knowledge of science and medicine not available in the first century, may offer additional insight concerning the possible mechanisms of Jesus' death.

When taken in concert, certain facts-the extensive and early testimony of both Christian proponents and opponents, and their universal acceptance of Jesus as a true historical figure; the ethic of the gospel writers, and the shortness of the time interval between the events and the extant manuscripts; and the confirmation of the gospel accounts by historians and archaeological findings-ensure a reliable testimony from which a modern medical interpretation of Jesus' death may be made.

Gethsemane

After Jesus and his disciples had observed the Passover meal in an upper room in a home in southwest Jerusalem, they traveled to the Mount of Olives, northeast of the city. (Owing to various adjustments in the calendar, the years of Jesus' birth and death remain controversial. However, it is likely that Jesus was born in either 4 or 6 BC and died in 30 AD. During the Passover observance in 30 AD, the Last Supper would have been observed on Thursday, April 6 [Nisan 13], and Jesus would have been crucified on Friday, April 7 [Nisan 14].) At nearby Gethsemane, Jesus, apparently knowing that the time of his death was near, suffered great mental anguish, and as described by the physician Luke, his sweat became like blood.

Although this is an exceedingly rare phenomenon, bloody sweat (hematidrosis or hemohidrosis) may occur in highly emotional states or in persons with bleeding disorders. As a result of hemorrhage into the sweat glands, the skin becomes fragile and tender. Luke's description supports the diagnosis of hematidrosis rather than eccrine chromidrosis (brown or yellow-green sweat) or stigmatization (blood oozing from the palms or elsewhere). Although some authors have suggested that hematidrosis produced hypovolemia, we agree with Bucklin that Jesus' actual blood loss probably was minimal. However, in the cold night air, it may have produced chills.

Jewish Trials

Soon after midnight, Jesus was arrested at Gethsemane by the temple officials and was taken first to Annas and then to Caiaphas, the Jewish high priest for that year. Between 1 AM and daybreak, Jesus was tried before Caiaphas and the political Sanhedrin and was found guilty of blasphemy. The guards then blindfolded Jesus, spat on him, and struck him in the face with their fists. Soon after daybreak, presumably at the temple, Jesus was tried before the religious Sanhedrin (with the Pharisees and the Sadducees) and again was found guilty of blasphemy, a crime punishable by death.

Roman Trials

Since permission for an execution had to come from the governing Romans, Jesus was taken early in the morning by the temple officials to the Praetorium of the Fortress of Antonia, the residence and governmental seat of Pontius Pilate, the procurator of Judea. However, Jesus was presented to Pilate not as a blasphemer but rather as a self-appointed king who would undermine the Roman authority. Pilate made no charges against Jesus and sent him to Herod Antipas, the tetrarch of Judea. Herod likewise made no official charges and then returned Jesus to Pilate. Again, Pilate could find no basis for a legal charge against Jesus, but the people persistently demanded crucifixion. Pilate finally granted their demand and handed over Jesus to be flogged (scourged) and crucified. (McDowell has reviewed the prevailing political, religious, and economic climates in Jerusalem at the time of Jesus' death, and Bucklin has described the various illegalities of the Jewish and Roman trials.)

Health of Jesus

The rigors of Jesus' ministry (that is, traveling by foot throughout Palestine) would have precluded any major physical illness or a weak general constitution. Accordingly, it is reasonable to assume that Jesus was in good physical condition before his walk to Gethsemane. However, during the 12 hours between 9 PM Thursday and 9 AM Friday, he had suffered great emotional stress (as evidenced by hematidrosis), abandonment by his closest friends (the disciples), and a physical beating (after the first Jewish trial). Also, in the setting of a traumatic and sleepless night, he had been forced to walk more than 2.5 miles (4.0 km) to and from the sites of the various trials. These physical and emotional factors may have rendered Jesus particularly vulnerable to the adverse herodynamic effects of the scourging.

SCOURGING

Scourging Practices

Flogging was a legal preliminary to every Roman execution, and only women and Roman senators or soldiers (except in cases of desertion) were exempt. The usual instrument was a short whip (flagrum or flagellum) with several single or braided leather thongs of variable lengths, in which small iron balls or sharp pieces of sheep bones were tied at intervals. Occasionally, staves also were used. For scourging, the man was stripped of his clothing, and his hands were tied to an upright post. The back, buttocks, and legs were flogged either by two soldiers (lictors) or by one who alternated positions. The severity of the scourging depended on the disposition of the lictors and was intended to weaken the victim to a state just short of collapse or death. After the scourging, the soldiers often taunted their victim.

Medical Aspects of Scourging

As the Roman soldiers repeatedly struck the victim's back with full force, the iron balls would cause deep contusions, and the leather thongs and sheep bones would cut into the skin and subcutaneous tissues. Then, as the flogging continued, the lacerations would tear into the underlying skeletal muscles and produce quivering ribbons of bleeding flesh. Pain and blood loss generally set the stage for circulatory shock. The extent of blood loss may well have determined how long the victim would survive on the cross.

Scourging of Jesus

At the Praetorium, Jesus was severely whipped. (Although the severity of the scourging is not discussed in the four gospel accounts, it is implied in one of the epistles [1 Peter 2:24]. A detailed work study of the ancient Greek text for this verse indicates that the scourging of Jesus was particularly harsh.) It is not known whether the number of lashes was limited to 39, in accordance with Jewish law. The Roman soldiers, amused that this weakened man had claimed to be a king, began to mock him by placing a robe on his shoulders, a crown of thorns on his head, and a wooden staff as a scepter in his right hand. Next, they spat on Jesus and struck him on the head with the wooden staff. Moreover, when the soldiers tore the robe from Jesus' back, they probably reopened the scourging wounds.

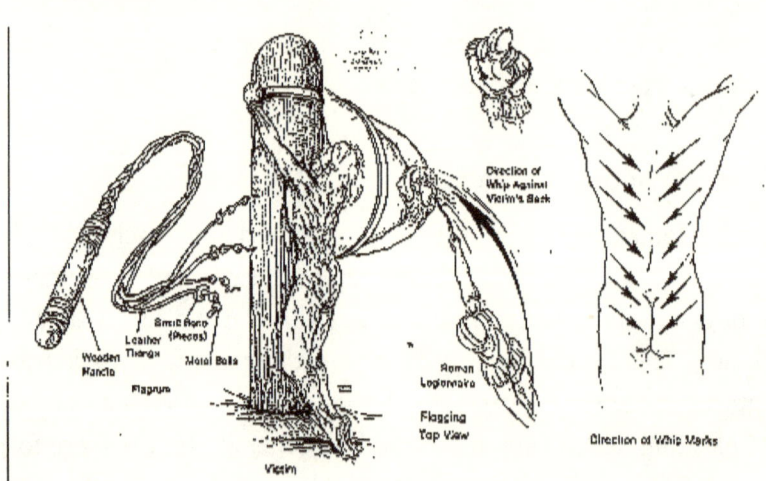

The severe scourging, with its intense pain and appreciable blood loss, most probably left Jesus in a pre-shock state. Moreover, hematidrosis had rendered his skin particularly tender. The physical and mental abuse meted out by the Jews and the Romans, as well as the lack of food, water, and sleep, also contributed to his generally weakened state. Therefore, even before the actual crucifixion, Jesus' physical condition was at least serious and possibly critical.

Crucifixion

Crucifixion Practices

Crucifixion probably first began among the Persians. Alexander the Great introduced the practice to Egypt and Carthage, and the Romans appear to have learned of it from the Carthaginians. Although the Romans did not invent crucifixion, they perfected it as a form of torture and capital punishment that was designed to produce a slow death with maximum pain and suffering. It was one of the most disgraceful and cruel methods of execution and usually was reserved only for slaves, foreigners, revolutionaries, and the vilest of criminals. Roman law usually protected Roman citizens from crucifixion, except perhaps in the case of desertion by soldiers.

In its earliest form in Persia, the victim was either tied to a tree or was tied to or impaled on an upright post, usually to keep the guilty victim's feet from touching holy ground. Only later was a true cross used; it was characterized by an upright post (stipes) and a horizontal crossbar (patibulum), and it had several variations. Although archaeological and historical evidence strongly indicates that the low Tau cross was preferred by the Romans in Palestine at the time of Christ, crucifixion practices often varied in a given geographic region and in accordance with the imagination of the executioners, and the Latin cross and other forms also may have been used.

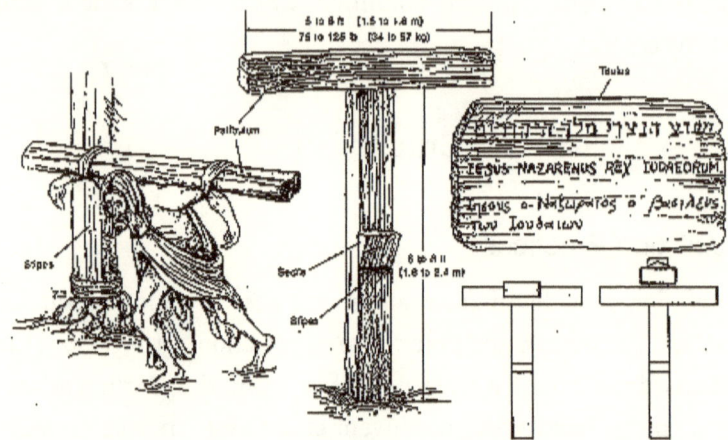

It was customary for the condemned man to carry his own cross from the flogging post to the site of crucifixion outside the city walls. He was usually naked unless this was prohibited by local customs. Since the weight of the entire cross was probably well over 300 lb. (136 kg), only the crossbar was carried. The patibulum, weighing 75 to 125 lb. (34 to 57 kg), was placed across the nape of the victim's neck and balanced along both shoulders. Usually, the outstretched arms then were tied to the crossbar. The processional to the site of crucifixion was led by a complete Roman military guard, headed by a centurion. One of the soldiers carried a sign (titulus) on which the condemned man's name and crime was displayed. Later, the titulus would be attached to the top of the cross. The Roman guard would not leave the victim until they were sure of his death.

Outside the city walls were permanently located the heavy upright wooden stipes, on which the patibulum would be secured. In the case of the Tau cross, this was accomplished by means of a mortise and tendon joint, with or without reinforcement by ropes. To prolong the crucifixion process, a horizontal wooden block or plank, serving as a crude seat (sedile or sedulum), often was attached midway down the stipes. Only very rarely, and probably later than the time of Christ, was an additional block (suppedaneum) employed for transfixion of the feet.

At the site of execution, by law, the victim was given a bitter drink of wine mixed with myrrh (gall) as a mild analgesic. The criminal was then thrown to the ground on his back, with his arms outstretched along the patibulum. The hands could be nailed or tied to the crossbar but nailing apparently was preferred by the Romans. The archaeological remains of a crucified body, found in an ossuary near Jerusalem and dating from the time of Christ, indicate that the nails were tapered iron spikes approximately 5 to 7 in (13 to 18 cm) long with a square shaft 3/8 in (1 cm) across. Furthermore, ossuary findings and the Shroud of Turin have documented that the nails commonly were driven through the wrists rather than the palms.

After both arms were fixed to the crossbar, the patibulum and the victim, together, were lifted onto the stipes. On the low cross, four soldiers could accomplish this relatively easily. However, on the tall cross, the soldiers used either wooden forks or ladders.

Next, the feet were fixed to the cross, either by nails or ropes. Ossuary findings and the Shroud of Turin suggest that nailing was the preferred Roman practice. Although the feet could be fixed to the sides of the stipes or to a wooden footrest (suppedaneum), they usually were nailed directly to the front of the stipes. To accomplish this, flexion of the knees may have been quite prominent, and the bent legs may have been rotated laterally.

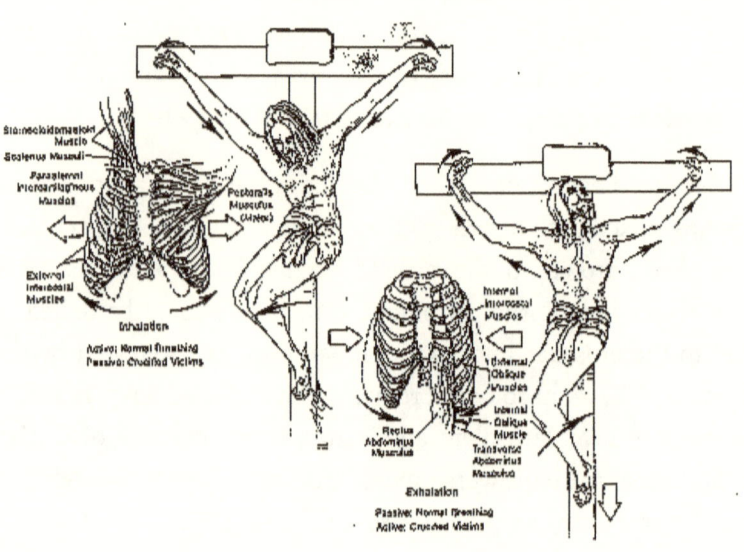

When the nailing was completed, the titulus was attached to the cross, by nails or cords, just above the victim's head. The soldiers and the civilian crowd often taunted and jeered the condemned man, and the soldiers customarily divided up his clothes among themselves. The length of survival generally ranged from three or four hours to three or four days and appears to have been inversely related to the severity of the scourging. However, even if the scourging had been relatively mild, the Roman soldiers could hasten death by breaking the legs below the knees (crucifragium or skelokopia).

Not uncommonly, insects would light upon or burrow into the open wounds or the eyes, ears, and nose of the dying and helpless victim, and birds of prey would tear at these sites. Moreover, it was customary to leave the corpse on the cross to be devoured by predatory animals. However, by Roman law, the family of the condemned could take the body for burial, after obtaining permission from the Roman judge.

Since no one was intended to survive crucifixion, the body was not released to the family until the soldiers were sure that the victim was dead. By custom, one of the Roman guards would pierce the body with a sword or lance. Traditionally, this had been considered a spear wound to the heart through the right side of the chest-a fatal wound probably taught to most Roman soldiers. The Shroud of Turin documents this form of injury. Moreover, the standard infantry spear, which was 5 to 6 ft (1.5 cm 1.8 m) long, could easily have reached the chest of a man crucified on the customary low cross.

Medical Aspects of Crucifixion

With a knowledge of both anatomy and ancient crucifixion practices, one may reconstruct the probable medical aspects of this form of slow execution. Each wound apparently was intended to produce intense agony, and the contributing causes of death were numerous.

The scourging prior to crucifixion served to weaken the condemned man and, if blood loss was considerable, to produce orthostatic hypertension and even hypovolemic shock. When the victim was thrown to the ground on his back, in preparation for transfixion of the hands, his scourging wounds most likely would become torn open again and contaminated with dirt. Furthermore, with each respiration, the painful scourging wounds would be scraped against the rough wood of the stipes. As a result, blood loss from the back probably would continue throughout the crucifixion ordeal.

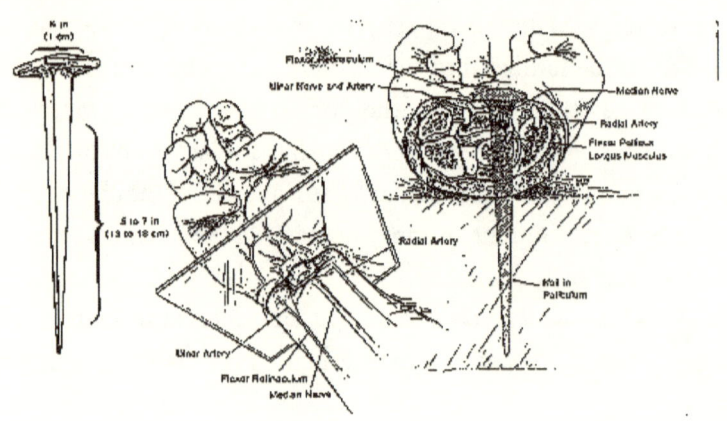

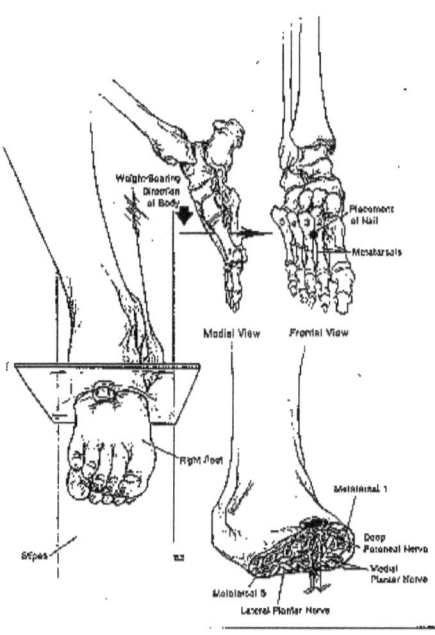

With arms outstretched but not taut, the wrists were nailed to the patibulum. It has been shown that the ligaments and bones of the wrist can support the weight of a body hanging from them, but the palms cannot. Accordingly, the iron spikes probably were driven between the radius and the carpals or between the two rows of carpal bones, either proximal to or through the strong bandlike flexor retinaculum and the various intercarpal ligaments. Although a nail in either location in the wrist might pass between the bony elements and thereby produce no fractures, the likelihood of painful periosteal injury would seem great. Furthermore, the driven nail would crush or sever the rather large sensorimotor median nerve. The stimulated nerve would produce excruciating bolts of fiery pain in both arms. Although the severed median nerve would result in paralysis of a portion of the hand, ischemic contractures and impalement of various ligaments by the iron spike might produce a claw-like grasp.

Most commonly, the feet were fixed to the front of the stipes by means of an iron spike driven through the first or second intermetatarsal space, just distal to the tarsometatarsal joint. It is likely that the deep peroneal nerve and branches of the medial and lateral plantar nerves would have been injured by the nails. Although scourging may have resulted in considerable blood loss, crucifixion per se was a relatively bloodless procedure, since no major arteries, other than perhaps the deep plantar arch, pass through the favored anatomic sites of transfixion.

The major pathophysiologic effect of crucifixion, beyond the excruciating pain, was a marked interference with normal respiration, particularly exhalation. The weight of the body, pulling down on the outstretched arms and shoulders, would tend to fix the intercostal muscles in an inhalation state and thereby hinder passive exhalation. Accordingly, exhalation was primarily diaphragmatic, and breathing was shallow. It is likely that this form of respiration would not suffice, and that hypercarbia would soon result. The onset of muscle cramps or tetanic contractions, due to fatigue and hypercarbia, would hinder respiration even further.

Adequate exhalation required lifting the body by pushing up on the feet and by flexing the elbows and adducting the shoulders. However, this maneuver would place the entire weight of the body on the tarsals and would produce searing pain. Furthermore, flexion of the elbows would cause rotation of the wrists about the iron nails and cause fiery pain along the damaged median nerves.

Lifting of the body would also painfully scrape the scourged back against the rough wooden stipes. Muscle cramps and paresthesias of the outstretched and uplifted arms would add to the discomfort. As a result, each respiratory effort would become agonizing and tiring and lead eventually to asphyxia.

The actual cause of death by crucifixion was multifactorial and varied somewhat with each case, but the two most prominent causes probably were hypovolemic shock and exhaustion asphyxia. Other possible contributing factors included dehydration, stress-induced arrhythmias, and congestive heart failure with the rapid accumulation of pericardial and perhaps pleural effusions. Crucifracture (breaking the legs below the knees), if performed, led to an asphyxic death within minutes. Death by crucifixion was, in every sense of the word, excruciating (Latin, excruciatus, or "out of the cross").

Crucifixion of Jesus

After the scourging and the mocking, at about 9 AM, the Roman soldiers put Jesus' clothes back on him and then led him and two thieves to be crucified. Jesus apparently was so weakened by the severe flogging that he could not carry the patibulum from the Praetorium to the site of crucifixion one third of a mile (600 to 650 m) away. Simon of Cyrene was summoned to carry Christ's cross, and the processional then made its way to Golgotha (or Calvary), an established crucifixion site.

Here, Jesus' clothes, except for a linen loincloth, again were removed, thereby probably reopening the scourging wounds. He then was offered a drink of wine mixed with myrrh (gall) but, after tasting it, refused the drink. Finally, Jesus and the two thieves were crucified. Although scriptural references are made to nails in the hands, these are not at odds with the archaeological evidence of wrist wounds, since the ancients customarily considered the wrist to be a part of the hand. The titulus was attached above Jesus' head. It is unclear whether Jesus was crucified on the Tau cross or the Latin cross; archaeological findings favor the former and early tradition the latter. The fact that Jesus later was offered a drink of wine vinegar from a sponge placed on the stalk of the hyssop plant (approximately 20 in, or 50 cm, long) strongly supports the belief that Jesus was crucified on the short cross.

The soldiers and the civilian crowd taunted Jesus throughout the crucifixion ordeal, and the soldiers cast lots for his clothing. Christ spoke seven times from the cross. Since speech occurs during exhalation, these short, terse utterances must have been particularly difficult and painful. At about 3 PM that Friday, Jesus cried out in a loud voice, bowed his head, and died. The Roman soldiers and onlookers recognized his moment of death.

Since the Jews did not want the bodies to remain on the crosses after sunset, the beginning of the Sabbath, they asked Pontius Pilate to order crucifracture to hasten the deaths of the three crucified men. The soldiers broke the legs of the two thieves, but when they came to Jesus and saw that he was already dead, they did not break his legs. Rather, one of the soldiers pierced his side, probably with an infantry spear, and produced a sudden flow of blood and water. Later that day, Jesus' body was taken down from the cross and placed in a tomb.

Death of Jesus

Two aspects of Jesus' death have been the source of great controversy, namely, the nature of the wound in his side and the cause of his death after only several hours on the cross. The gospel of John describes the piercing of Jesus' side and emphasizes the sudden flow of blood and water. Some authors have interpreted the flow of water to be ascites or urine, from an abdominal midline perforation of the bladder. However, the Greek word (pleura) used by John clearly denoted laterality and often implied the ribs. Therefore, it seems probable that the wound was in the thorax and far away from the abdominal midline.

Although the side of the wound was not designated by John, it traditionally has been depicted on the right side. Supporting this tradition is the fact that a large flow of blood would be more likely with a perforation of the distended and thin-walled right atrium or ventricle than the thick-walled and contracted left ventricle. Although the side of the wound may never be established with certainty, the right seems more probable than the left.

Some of the skepticism in accepting John's description has arisen from the difficulty in explaining, with medical accuracy, the flow of both blood and water. Part of this difficulty has been based on the assumption that the blood appeared first, then the water. However, in the ancient Greek, the order of words generally denoted prominence and not necessarily a time sequence. Therefore, it seems likely that John was emphasizing the prominence of blood rather than its appearance preceding the water.

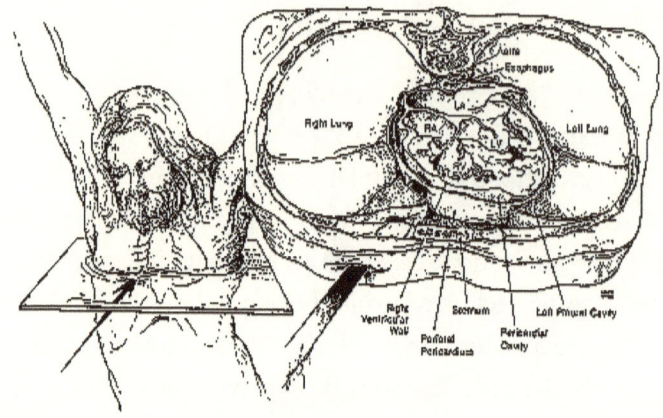

Therefore, the water probably represented serous pleural and pericardial fluid, and would have preceded the flow of blood and been smaller in volume than the blood. Perhaps in the setting of hypovolemia and impending acute heart failure, pleural and pericardial effusions may have developed and would have added to the volume of apparent water. The blood, in contrast, may have originated from the right atrium or the right ventricle or perhaps from a hemopericardium.

Jesus' death after only three to six hours on the cross surprised even Pontius Pilate. The fact that Jesus cried out in a loud voice and then bowed his head and died suggests the possibility of a catastrophic terminal event. One popular explanation has been that Jesus died of cardiac rupture. In the setting of the scourging and crucifixion, with associated hypovolemia, hypoxemia, and perhaps an altered coagulable state, friable non-infective thrombotic vegetations could have formed on the aortic or mitral valve. These then could have dislodged and embolized into the coronary circulation and thereby produced an acute transmural myocardial infarction. Thrombotic valvular vegetations have been reported to develop under analogous acute traumatic conditions. Rupture of the left ventricular free wall may occur, though uncommonly, in the first few hours following infarction.

However, another explanation may be more likely. Jesus' death may have been hastened simply by his state of exhaustion and by the severity of the scourging, with its resultant blood loss and pre-shock state. The fact that he could not carry his patibulum supports this interpretation. The actual cause of Jesus' death, like that of other crucified victims, may have been multifactorial and related primarily to hypovolemic shock, exhaustion asphyxia, and perhaps acute heart failure. A fatal cardiac arrhythmia may have accounted for the apparent catastrophic terminal event.

Thus, it remains unsettled whether Jesus died of cardiac rupture or of cardiorespiratory failure. However, the important feature may be not how he died but rather whether he died. Clearly, the weight of historical and medical evidence indicates that Jesus was dead before the wound to his side was inflicted and supports the traditional view that the spear, thrust between his right ribs, probably perforated not only the right lung but also the pericardium and heart and thereby ensured his death. Accordingly, interpretations based on the assumption that Jesus did not die on the cross appear to be at odds with modern medical knowledge.

WHAT MUST I DO TO BE SAVED?

References

- Ancient Hebrew – Aramaic Bible
- Lamsa Bible English Peshitta Translation - George Lamsa's famous Peshitta New Testament English translation
- The Tyndale Bible
- The Cost of Discipleship – Dietrich Bonhoeffer
- The Church – Hans Kung
- The Mind of Jesus by William Barclay
- History of the Early Church by Norbert Brox
- Saddharma-pundarika-sutra (Lotus Sutra) – Courtesy of Soka Gakkai International

WHAT MUST I DO TO BE SAVED?

The whole of Christian philosophy lies in this, our understanding that all our hope is placed in God, who freely gives us all things through Jesus his son, that we were redeemed by his death and engrafted through baptism with his body, that we might be dead to the desires of this world and live by his teaching and example, and that we may ever advance from one virtue to another, yet in such a way that we claim nothing for ourselves, but ascribe any good we do to God.

WHAT MUST I DO TO BE SAVED?